BEYOND
WORDS

REFLECTIONS ON OUR
JOURNEY TO INCLUSION

ISBN: 978-0-615-33391-5

In cooperation with Lightning Source, La Vergne, TN 37086

Book Designed and Illustrated by Grace Choi

Printed in the United States of America

BEYOND WORDS

REFLECTIONS ON OUR JOURNEY TO INCLUSION

WRITTEN BY
DIANE LINDER

IN CONSULTATION WITH AND
EDITED BY
MAYA MEMLING

ILLUSTRATIONS BY
GRACE CHOI

Sun Hat Press

To My
Two Beautiful Boys
and
To My Mother.

Contents

In Acknowledgement

This book would not be a book at all without Maya Memling. With great patience and humor she has nourished it from the start. Her keen eye and psychological acumen have made it much better than I ever thought it could be.

Grace Choi gave her talents to the design and illustrations with great generosity of spirit.

I credit the memory of my father, Ralph Linder, for instilling in me a tremendous respect for the written word.

Brigitte Bentele was one of my first readers. There is no one else who could have simultaneously offered positive support, in the very same moments as she gave astute suggestions for restructuring the entire narrative.

Debbie Oberlander read early versions with an enthusiasm that helped me keep going.

Don Behrman, cousin and friend, read the book in one sitting, into the early hours of the morning. His heartfelt comments were a source of great encouragement to me.

And finally, I must thank David, my very best friend and partner in life, who read every version and listened to new sentences at all hours of the night.

1   Nancy and Apple Hill

Summer 1996, East Sullivan, New Hampshire

Some assume that having a child with special needs changes one's life. For me it was not my child who changed me as much as it was the people I encountered through my son. Some of these people taught me more than I knew I could learn. My journey began long before I became a parent, and almost a year before I met my husband, David. It began when I met Nancy.

It was early summer, the grass still young and light, the air still sweet with the blossoms of spring. I arrived early in the day for chamber music camp. Dobbs, the director and double bass player, gave me the traditional welcome hug, a hug so strong I nearly toppled. There was extra enthusiasm that day as he told me his sister-in-law, Nancy, would be joining me in a trio for voice, clarinet, and piano. I was to be the clarinetist, joining with her voice in song. He told me she had an incredible voice. He did not tell me that twelve years later she would play such a major part in my life.

Apple Hill is an idyllic retreat for amateur chamber musicians of all ages. Nestled between rolling hills, it lies several miles outside of a small town. The closest store, a tiny convenience shop, is a three mile walk away. Participants sleep in wooden cabins tucked around the campus. Meals and baths take place in a large central barn. None of the doors have locks, a feature most unique for me, coming from a lifetime in New York City. It took me a few summers to relax enough to leave my keys and wallet loosely piled in the cubby with my name. Once I made it to that point, time there was unlike any other time in my year. Apple Hill was a place that transformed me for the ten days I was there. It was a visit to another state of mind, a place where there were no worries, only pleasures.

At Apple Hill, I saw the universe for the first time. Deep into the evening, I would look up at the sky and there it was sparkling right in front of my eyes. At first, I would see just a few stars but as I'd lie beneath, the sky would slowly reveal the treasures that are hidden from those who dwelt in cities. I remember spending hours each night on my back, my clothes soaked with dew by early morning, my head filled with wonder by dawn.

We spent the days in our musical groups, matched only by our musical inclinations. There was an incredible diversity to the population on every level, yet when we sat down to play we were equals. Children worked on trios alongside adults, physicists with writers, even citizens from countries at war. We were united by a common goal. We were there to play music, to listen to each other, to play together, to reach beyond ourselves. The coaches, chamber musicians themselves, had a unique approach. They expected us to rise to a level of musicality that was not bound by our abilities. Session after session, it was clear that they believed that we could find our voice as a group. Perhaps of all the coaches Dobbs worked this magic the best. He described in words and motions, and even in the strength of his silences how we could touch the music and move past the technical challenges, regardless of our level of skill. We learned not to focus on the notes, not to think about our difficulties, but to listen to each other, to hear beyond the notes, to be open to all the sounds as we played. And we did. Day after day, year after year, groups came through and played so beautifully that it seemed as if the composers were there in the woods, silently conducting, humming, and dancing as we reached for the melodies and harmonies they left outlined for us on the score.

We took breaks now and then to rest our weary embouchures, and our tired wrists. During these breaks, some took to the grassy hilltops; others found the shade beneath the trees. The few hours between rehearsals were for me a chance to get to know my fellow musicians. At Apple Hill the ten days was a mini-lifetime, and often by day two relationships began to form. The whole communal nature of a common bathroom, showers without curtains, and unlocked cubbies, made for boundaries to fall quickly and friendships to form fast.

Nancy came late, tired and wet from a driving rain that falls wetter and steadier on that hill than anywhere else I have been. She stumbled into the communal barn drenched and tired. Within minutes she told me she did not want to be there. Days before she flew home from Guatemala with a two year old little boy she and her husband had adopted. She did not realize the timing would work out as it did, and she begged her husband's brother to let her out of her commitment. She had an older child with multiple disabilities requiring much supervision and a toddler new to the family.

She wanted to be at home nesting with her family. Dobbs was adamant that she attend the session as planned. So instead of nesting she found herself wet, and worn, and facing ten days of sleeping in a cabin in the woods. We found out we were bunkmates, straddling thirty at the time, and we were put together in a cabin for the "older ladies."

By bedtime we were friends. Not my usual style to bond so quickly even here on the Hill, I tumbled into this friendship fast. We made each other laugh. She came with responsibilities greater than I had ever known but she let me entertain her. She laughed at my attempts to keep the mosquitoes away, and the sun out of my eyes. Though close in age we were at vastly different places in life. I was single, had a simple job, and was only remotely concerned with filling my life with more than it had. She was pursuing a PhD in psychology, had two children, a ten year old marriage and a host of lifelong adventures before her. Yet we understood each other. Even then it was clear she represented the future and I the past. We were both a little neurotic, creative, and insightful. She was daring and I was reserved. Our conversations quickly took all forms. We talked about the most serious of issues and the zaniest as well. We also planned a hilarious skit for the talent show. One day we laughed so hard we cried for almost a full hour, and I can not recall about what.

We were serious when we rehearsed. Her life had a richness mine lacked, but she was able to pull me in and together we reached musical heights I have not been to since. We worked for ten days on six German songs by Ludwig Spohr. I remember working on *Weigenleid* (Lullaby) and also *Das Heimliche Leid* (The Secret Song). They are both beautiful songs filled with tenderness and yearning. Nancy took the words and sang them with such that care even in rehearsal I was often close to tears. Nancy swept me up into her world of love, loss, joy, and pain. With her voice she brought me to where she was and we made music from the start. We worked, we shaped, we sculpted, but the foundation was there from the beginning. To this day, whenever I play those pieces, inside I am playing them still with her.

The final concert took place in the communal barn. Often barefoot, campers would sit in the loft, toes dangling above our heads. As the final notes fell, hands would clap and feet would thunder as they rumbled against the soft wooden beams that held the loft in place. The silence as we played was a deep milky silence rippled only by the breeze, soft birds, and insects exotic to my ears. The thunder of the bare feet above our heads seconds after we finished reached an intensity new to me, even after twelve summers of concerts in that barn.

When the session ended we had formed a small group of friends, mainly professional woman in our early thirties. We exchanged contact information and vowed to stay in touch. I knew chances were we would not, but I went through the last day ritual of hugs and promises. Somehow after all these years, I accepted that time there allowed connections to form that life often erased. Most of my Apple Hill friendships are with me in my heart. They have shaped me and changed me but they are in my past. After a few letters during the year, an occasional call, most of them invariably tapered off to a sweet memory inside.

My friendship with Nancy was different. Nancy and I stayed in touch. We sustained the friendship over e-mail for twelve years. We e-mailed each day for a while and then our correspondence slowed, but never ended. Months would pass without words and then one of us would reach out. I was often the one to initiate, as she was busier, getting a PhD, having a surprise pregnancy the next year, and then raising three children. She was very involved in securing an inclusive education for her oldest child. She fought the district for years and won, and was very proud of her accomplishments. She became an advocate for inclusion, often attending district meetings for other families. She co-authored a chapter about her experiences in a book with her husband. I was always interested in her achievements but never believed they would impact my life. Our correspondence was varied always, very serious at times to completely silly at others. Even over e-mail she made me laugh out loud, and I often had to wait until after work to open her responses.

The year after we met, I met my husband. She coached me via e-mail on dating and then early marriage. Over e-mail I could share things I might not share otherwise. Her friendship was and still is the only friendship I developed and sustained over e-mail. We became close. She almost sang at my wedding, but a series of spring viruses kept her home. When I became pregnant she coached me again, and then I even got a little advice on breastfeeding. Once I left my full time job, I looked forward to more frequent contact since I had my days free. As soon as Benny would take his nap, I went to my computer. She gave me a little intellectual fulfillment during some long and dreary days.

When my son turned two it became clear that he, too, had some special needs, delays in speech and motor planning. I shared all our ventures with Nancy, and she lent a supportive voice by e-mail. As he approached school age, Nancy kept bringing me back to her story, which I only dimly related to mine. Her son had vastly different issues and I did not connect to her message. She then sent me the chapters from the book she co-authored on inclusion and sent me video clips of her son at school. I was proud of her and him, but did not see out of the box for Benny. I could sense a growing frustration in her, and only now do I understand why.

As a teacher in the city in which we lived I knew inclusion was not a possibility for Benny. Our city system was too crowded, too complicated, and too broken to even begin the debate. I convinced myself that Benny needed a segregated setting. I told myself it would be temporary, that by second grade he would catch up. Nancy tried to warn me that he would not have access to the same curriculum. She told me how easy integration is when the child is young, how far early integration goes to promote eventual acceptance, and how much harder it is to integrate later on. I disregarded her words. There was nothing I could do, I told myself. She did not understand my city as I did and that was that. Our correspondence tapered but I could not let go completely.

I am very fortunate that her words stayed with me even though I tried to shut them out. I am very lucky that I met her and managed to hang on to her for so many years. She is one of several people that joined together in the end and helped me save my son. She gave me a vision of a type of education I did not have access to even though I am a teacher myself. I am very grateful that I met her and that she persisted in her mission to educate me, even though I was not as open as I should have been.

What follows is our story, with a spotlight on those around us, the therapists, the teachers, the administrators, and even friends and students from my distant past, who have danced both with and around us. For better and worse they have helped us to shape a world in which we can live. I began this as a project for myself. As I wrote I began to think that perhaps this could be useful for other parents. This is a study of choices, of decisions, and of those educators who helped me find my voice as we all waited for Benny to find his.

2 The Birth

I learned I was pregnant one September morning at 5 A.M. It was the first day of classes in the middle school where I had been teaching mathematics for eleven years. Even after teaching successfully, this day made me nervous. After just a few years I noticed that the first few moments of the first day seemed to set the tone for the entire year. Each class, a complex blend of personalities and talents, took on a form almost instantaneously. Two sections of the same grade could come together to create two entirely different experiences when defined as a class. Some classes were places of complete comfort, while in others, a tension hung in the air, like raindrops waiting to fall. With some classes there was always a communal desire to push ahead, with others a omnipresent pull to hold back. I was not sure how much I as the teacher determined this mix, but I felt in some way, the first day was my most important. The first day was my downbeat from which the rest of the year would unfold like a symphony.

I tried to come prepared with something a little new and a little different. I wanted an activity that would grab them, challenge them, entice them from the start to be actively engaged. I rarely slept the night before, turning questions around in my head, trying to be ready with all variations, ready to suit the needs of my students. And so that is how I came to be up, with the birds, holding three pairs of pink lines up to the light in my tiny studio apartment bathroom.

Although I had two previous miscarriages, I knew this one would take. From the very beginning it felt secure, and I felt confident. I left my apartment early, and I went to the gym, then to the fruit store, and finally to my school. One hour later, during an algebra lesson, we all learned together that the towers had fallen.

I could not reach David, and I imagined him trapped in the subway tunnel beneath the rubble. I ran from one pay phone to another until I reached my mother. She had spoken to David and he had made it safely to his Brooklyn school. Still, I could not stop crying. I was scared and I felt guilty, guilty for caring so for an embryo while so many lay dead as we spoke.

How could I care so for a possibility of life while the certainty of death filled the sky with darkness? Yet, what else could I do but cling tightly to what we all had become after those moments; precarious, possibilities of life.

The events of the day colored my thoughts for the entire nine months. Questions filled up all the spaces in my head like a thick morning fog. I wondered if I would love this child more, or differently as a result of this circumstance. I asked myself who I was to bring a child into a world so disorganized, and so fractured. Maybe some of these questions pass through the mind of every expectant parent in any given year, but the coupling of this tragic day with the expectation of parenthood made these thoughts more pronounced. I was, at the time, so acutely aware of the damage one human could cause, that the responsibility ahead to keep this child safe seemed daunting. Each day I looked over my broken city, and I made all sorts of promises to myself, and to the universe. I vowed that I would help this child become a person who would help repair the world. I tried to convince myself that this child might possibly make this world a little gentler.

Benny arrived three weeks early. His birth was long and difficult. As he began to make his way out, the sun, rising over the East River, spread dancing shadows upon the solid brick wall just a few feet from my window. For a moment I became absorbed by the swiftly moving designs, as reds were spreading into purples, blues, bouncing off the river, were melting into what seemed like soft yellow clouds, but then he was out and he was quiet. He did not cry. Some bell must have sounded in the hall and doctors swarmed in and around him, patting him, tapping him, turning him upside down and right side up, and I watched unable to breath myself until he could. When he finally made a small sound, we relaxed, and they placed him by my side. I looked at him and understood; I understood things that in the near future would fail to make sense. It was an unusual sensation, almost as if for a moment my past and future came together with an unusual clarity. Within the narrow confines of this moment I was able to peer into the expanse of time that spread ahead of us both. I looked over this expanse and became conscious of a monumental and dazzling beauty dotted with regions of an intense throbbing darkness. As I strained to see the details, the expanse contracted and left me where I belonged – in the present, with a 6 pound baby boy on my chest, a doctor placing two hundred stitches in my bottom, and the sound of David on the telephone, telling the grandparents that Benny had been born.

From the very start he never failed to attract attention. In between trips to the Neonatal Intensive Care Unit to explore why he could not swallow, I would catch the nurses huddled around him combing his thick hair from side to side. When he was a baby I was stopped all the time, as everyone demanded to look closely at this child swaddled in blankets somehow even then radiating something indescribable into the atmosphere.

His love of music was there from the start. I first took my clarinet from the case when he was six weeks old. It had been a long hiatus for me and my tone was thin, my fingers clumsy. Benny had been lying on the bed when I began to play *Mozart's Clarinet Concerto*. As the first notes sounded, his eyes opened  wide, and his body wiggled in time to the music. He listened to all three movements, distressed only when I paused to turn a page, or fix my reed, or take a much needed breath. He was soothed only by the continuation of sound. Once he could roll over, he would roll the length of the living room to position himself right under the bell of my clarinet. Our days were full with pleasures: we took long morning walks, ate lunch while reading good books, and then relaxed with some classical music.

Until the age of two we assumed he was on his own time clock. He missed virtually every milestone in the baby book, but he was easygoing, smiled early, loved his family, and enjoyed a good book. He had a wisdom about him that told me he would be fine.

By the age of two his sunny demeanor began to turn. He was frustrated. A late walker, his instability as well as his inability to produce words or even "word approximations" prompted us to call in our first set of evaluators.

3 First Evaluators

I stand at the oversized window in our living room and I strain to see the people coming down the block. I see two women in black carrying clipboards and I call to David. The evaluators are here, I say, and he comes running. By the time we both look again they are in the lobby ringing the bell, and the process has begun.

I answer the door almost excited inside. I hold five month old Adam, and I call to Benny who has just turned two. I make it seem like they are here for a play date. I tell him they will have toys. He scampers out to meet them. I look at him, so sunny and smiley. Even though I have accepted that fact that he is delayed in speech I am sure that they will see how brilliant he is. If they do not think he is brilliant, then at least they'll see how personable he is. I wonder if he will qualify for services at all when they see how he can identify twenty-six tunes on his alphabet bus.

They come in with forms to sign and questions to ask. They leave their toys in boxes which Benny runs to open. He finds stacking cups which he twirls and spoons which he balances on top of the towers he eventually makes. Their questions begin to make me tense, they hint of large disturbances, ones I read about in special education class just a few years earlier. I try to remember which disability goes with which question, but in the end I say yes to so many questions that it is not until later with my text book in hand that I can pin down their suspicions. Some questions they answer themselves. If I disagree they note that, and I fear now they are judging me. I am sure he does not toe walk, yet they catch him on his toes reaching for a toy up high on a shelf, and so they mark yes.

Finally they try to engage him, and he is not interested in their games. He has his own agenda now. I think to myself that if they had come in and greeted him with warmth he would be their friends by now. I suspect that he knows already I do not like these people. They keep trying. With high sing song voices they cajole him to play their way. They mark down that he fails to use the spoon to eat pretend food out of an empty bowl. They can not get him to mimic a dog's bark or a cat's meow. He does not even point to familiar animals in the books they have with them. They keep glancing at me and David, asking us every few seconds if a particular behavior is typical. I sense it does not matter what I answer and already I do not know how to answer. Yes it is typical for him when he is agitated, but not typical for him when he is calm. So how do I respond? I am dizzy already with doubts, and then they tell me he needs intensive help. They suggest I send him to a center-based school, a school he would ride a bus to and from each day. He runs into my arms as they speak, even though he just scored in the 1st percentile for his age on the receptive language assessment. They suggest I enroll him in their school right now so that they can begin to help him develop more appropriate behaviors. I want to throw them out of my home. I want to step back one hour to a time when my life was sweet and my son was fine. I am convinced that they are creating these issues. As these thoughts pass through my head, I realize that I am paranoid and very much in denial. This realization momentarily prevents me from assessing whether or not this agency is competent enough to work with our family.

Before the evaluators leave they tell me that they want an occupation-al therapist, as well as a physical therapist "to take a look at him." I imagine Benny passive on an exam table, while two more "experts" come to view his body. The social worker ties up the meeting with a monotonic summary, a long run-on sentence, a certain amount of sympathy. "Maybe" she begins, "this is all new to you and you are surprised to hear these things, or maybe you sensed for a while that he had serious problems. In any case, this has not been easy for you." She picks herself up from the couch where she sat still for the hour plus, and all together they make their way out to the street. Deep down we know he struggles, deep down we know there are problems and we know he needs help. I feel detached from it all. I do not like these people but I am sure that it is because I do not like what they say. I tell myself I would not like anyone who delivered this news to me. They seem cold, but I tell myself maybe they have to be. Like the bitter penicillin I drank daily for my ear infection at age six, I swallow their words and I let their agency begin to work with my son. I believe them when they tell me that the pain is part of the package.

Over the next few weeks, David and I argue every day. He resents my negativity. I can not contain it. He says I am contradictory. The team works on setting up several therapists to come to the home and begin to heal my child. David suggests that if I really don't trust this team we should move on. I ask if he wants to and he does not. I am reluctant to prolong the agony. I want to start Benny's therapy soon. I am afraid I will dislike everyone in the field. He finds me irrational and it makes me angry. I hope that one day it will all make sense.

4 The Team Comes to Work

A few weeks later the therapists arrive at our door. They come every day for thirty minutes each. The speech therapist, Judy, is a mature woman with a body that seems to have aged rapidly and recently. Not yet comfortable in her new form, she walks with an awkward gait. She is a large woman whose clothes are tasteful and drape loosely over the extra pounds that have been deposited over the years. Her personality reflects the tension of her body. In her eyes lies an intelligent playfulness, while in her mind a rigid slothfulness has taken root. There are moments when in passing conversation she makes brilliant observations about Benny, but repeatedly fails to utilize these in practice. She carries an oversized tote filled with toys and props. Many of these toys are dusty, old, covered with years of finger prints, a history of all the other children she has tried to help over the years. Often she can not locate a particular toy from one session to the next. They fall carelessly into the tote and remain lost until they resurface months later. There is randomness to her time with Benny, yet she insists on a certain structure from him. Blaming her achy body she asks us to have him strapped into his high chair for each session. She requests to work in the darkest dreariest part of the apartment to minimize distractions. He is unhappy from the start. Her raspy voice sings his favorite songs, to him and he covers his ears. I worry that her nonstop talking leaves little space for him to respond. I question her gently and she tells me that she is modeling proper conversation. Her ability to appreciate his wit and intelligence endears her to me and for a short while I overlook her incapacity to form a relationship of substance with him.

His special education teacher, Amy, presents as a woman with competence who does not want to get too involved. A bouncy rotund redhead, she comes to the door with up to date varied toys and games. Our conversations are brief. She has little interest in my opinions or questions. She pegs me immediately as a dreamer with unrealistic hopes for Benny. Nevertheless she falls quickly and deeply for him. Her continual habit of arriving six minutes late and leaving six minutes early leaves her only eighteen minutes with him, but their time together is charged and focused. Her rules seem random and her goals occasionally contradictory, yet she brings out an enthusiasm in him not often seen. She is gentle with him, and only after he has run into another room does she corner me with her disdainful eye and tell me more of the weaknesses she was able to uncover.

As the weeks pass by, Benny becomes more and more resistant to Judy. He begins to cry as soon as she rings the bell, and refuses to comply with any of her requests. He passes the time, strapped in his chair, spitting and drooling, two habits he began in session with her. She continues to tell me that she sees intelligence and personality in him, and her comments numb the pain that has become a constant for me. I hold on to her for this reason alone. I know her words mean little in light of the disastrous relationship she has developed with him, but I need them for now. This need sickens me. Hidden away, tucked like the blueprint in a tiny seed, I begin to suspect that this dependence could grow into our downfall.

With Amy, Benny has a relationship. He often fails to complete or even to begin the tasks that she brings for him to do, but he is engaged. When I watch them work, I see that he is learning a skill that she has not been trying to teach. She brings blocks to sort, beads to string, and games so he will learn the art of taking turns. Benny is not interested in any of that. Instead he works to change her, and he succeeds. She comes with her plan and he gets her to play his way, Little by little she takes more risks, little by little he softens her. At first she complies for a minute or two, but by a month's time, she follows his lead for longer. She laughs with him; she begins to see him as a child with a personality, who can communicate without the words she waits for each day. She does not admit this, and in her log, which I must sign, she writes only about his failures. I do not care any longer what I sign, and I have already learned to let her words roll off. They roll easily, soggy and heavy with doom, they pool at my feet. I see that they are both growing in ways she may never articulate and for now that is all I need to see. Still I yearn for a therapist who has meaningful goals, a teacher who can relate to us both, someone with whom I can be honest with, whose words I do not have to dodge, but instead will nourish me, and not just provide a temporary anesthesia.

5 Jennifer Comes to Town

Jennifer always comes to town around Chanukah time. Her parents live a few blocks from our apartment, and we spend as much time as possible together when she is here. This year the tone is dark. Jennifer is a person who solves problems, who analyzes everything. She will stay up all night to research an issue, and in the end she can change national policy. This week she is frustrated because we cannot find answers to the questions raised by Benny's delays. Over the phone she is supportive, and strong, but in person she can't contain her worry. It is written all over her face and we can't seem to find a way to laugh anymore.

I met Jennifer in summer of 1981. Like Nancy, my relationship with Jennifer began with music. We were campers together at The Usdan Center for Music and Art in Dix Hills, Long Island. We were in the orchestra; she was the principal flutist and I was the principal clarinetist. That summer we worked on *Schubert's Unfinished Symphony*. The symphony starts with eight bars of a dark, brooding cello and bass line. The violins then lighten the mood with four bars of crisp sixteenth notes. Then the clarinet and oboe join in together in unison with a gentle melody. This melody returns again a few measures later, this time with the clarinet and flute in unison.

This was my first meeting with Jennifer. We played our part over and over trying to achieve a blend in our sound that was complete. We were to sound like one. Mr. Rudolf, our conductor, would yell to us, over the violins, to create a new sound, a clariflute, a flutinet, he would say, and we would try. We were young that summer, new to the orchestra. I know there were moments when we achieved this blending, but I am not sure how long we were able to sustain. Still we felt it; we touched it, if only for a moment or two. It is not often that one can trace back to the beginning of a friendship, to the point before words become part of it all.

We shared a long bus ride that summer to and from camp, but we never spoke. I already knew she was one of the smartest and most talented students at the neighboring Junior High. I remember thinking how nice she seemed, how kind. She had none of the arrogance I had already learned to expect with the top performers in school.

The next year we both found ourselves heading to Stuyvesant High School. We each came with a group of friends from our respective junior highs and remained tightly cocooned with our pack for the first year. By the beginning of our second year our groups began to merge. We shared a long commute from our outer borough neighborhood to the old 14th Street location of Stuyvesant High. Jennifer and I were the last of the friends to find each other. Somewhat less social, we missed some of the parties and events that brought various groups of students together. She often stayed home to study, and I was more interested in practicing my clarinet than venturing out late. One day we found each other on a busy street, in the center of the town in which we lived. Though few words had been exchanged until that chance meeting, we could not stop talking once we began. After that we sat together on the train each morning. We had so much to go over. We had a few years of shared observations that we had never discussed.

If not for Jennifer's amazingly warm demeanor and genuine interest in my conversation, I would have felt completely intimidated by her. She was and is brilliant. She would explain advanced calculus to me as we hung together on a pole in the middle of a crowded train. She would explain the GNP and other terms from economics which never sank in otherwise. And she had a sense for people and their motivations that was tremendous. In this area I could keep up a bit and together we analyzed everyone in our world. While wondering many a year what exactly a best friend was, I think I figured it out when I met Jennifer. She was and still is a person I can call four times a day if I need to. She is a person who is way smarter than I am but has still not accepted that fact.

She went to Harvard and I to Barnard and from then on we have barely spent more than a weekend in the same city. Nevertheless throughout all these years, well over twenty, we have spoken several times each week. She would call at any time of day or night, and during the dating years often did. While I generally kept to a bed by ten routine for most of my life, I would answer a call from her at any time. Neither of us made a move in a relationship without reviewing it with one another. I accepted her advice without question. After I had only a handful of dates with David, Jennifer flew in from Pittsburgh to meet him. She suspected the relationship was serious and knew her approval was as essential as my mother's. Had she found him lacking any quality she felt I needed, he would have been sent packing. David knew this too, and later described for me the tremendous anxiety he experienced before and during our first dinner all together.

She became a disability rights lawyer and I became a teacher and a mother.

She is now deputy Legal Director of the Bazelon Center for Mental Health Law, and I am often cleaning someone's tushy when she calls.

These days she works advocating for more integrative settings for persons with mental illness. She also has recently been asked to help craft legislation that would restore the protections of the Americans with Disabilities Act. (ADA)

She married Ken, a large and playful man who works with autistic children. Together they are the guardians of my two. He is warm and kind and when they visit he scoops them both up in his big arms and keeps them entertained for the duration of their visit. In that time, Jennifer and I can catch up. The tone of our time together had not changed much, over all these years, until this visit.

This time, she sits on the couch during Benny's therapy sessions and as I try to keep up a conversation, she keeps an ear to the kitchen while he "works" with his therapists. She tells me that something is wrong, that he should be happier. She forces me to listen closer than I had been. I hear Judy trying to get him to say "raisin." Judy introduced him to them and when she saw how much he liked them she decided to use them as a motivating reward. She holds them out in front of him and tells him over and over to say "raisin," she models it again and again, but Benny there are only sounds of discomfort. When "raisin" fails to work, she fishes out a toy he enjoys, and holds it just out of reach. She tells him to say the word, or even just to make a sound approximating the word, and then she will give it to him. He lets a few grunts and groans escape, which over the course of the session crescendo into a loud wail. By the time she leaves his face is hot and red. Jennifer reminds me of how joyfully he plays with Ken. She tells me how much fun Ken has at times even with severely autistic kids. I am so tired I don't want to listen. She suggests we find a top notch team of therapists. She reminds me that he is my child and in her voice there is disbelief that I am allowing him to be so mistreated. She is pained and worried for Benny. I know she is right but she makes me a little angry. I do not know where to turn for better help. I explain how we are waiting to see an expert, but the wait is long. I tell myself that she doesn't understand, and probably this is true, but I know that does not mean that she is wrong. She has a pasty worried look on her face all weekend. She is stuck because she has no answers and this is not a state she is often in.

Inside I resent her commentary. After all these years of friendship, to myself, I accuse her of overstepping her role. Even though we have shared opinions on the most sensitive of issues, this time, for the first time, I want her to be quiet. I want to enjoy her company, I want a break from the agony, and I do not want her to tell me that I have to do more, because I do not know what more I can do. I feel trapped, and as she suggests to me that the situation needs work, I feel a helplessness settling in. I do not like how this feels and so I try to block her out.

I am not even sure whether I should share with Jennifer our visit from the social worker in early November. I know once I go into that, our entire weekend will be taken over by this. I tell her, and we slide down the slippery slide together.

On Election Day, the social worker from the agency came for what was supposed to be a routine visit. She sat through a therapy session shaking her head, rolling her eyes, and writing voluminous notes. Then she sat on the floor of my living room and told me there was not a doubt in anyone's mind that Benny was autistic and retarded. She told me that she was waiting for the right time to tell me, that she knew it would be difficult for me to accept. I thought I heard a touch of sadism in her voice as she spoke. She seemed to me a bit too eager to be the one to tell me. At the same time I could not picture the type of person I could hear this from with graciousness. I held back my distrust, I held in my anger. I was sure that they were the by-product of my denial. I wanted to be strong, I wanted to be kind, and so I offered her some fruit. We sat together as she ate some grapes, and discussed the future. Inside my head there was darkness. I felt like I was losing my sight. My eyes told me that the social worker was a monster, and the therapists were going to kill us, but a voice told me that I had to listen, to accept, to trust, and so I tried. I let the social worker pretend to comfort me. I agreed to more therapy sessions with this team. Before the social worker left she handed me a card from a neurologist she worked with. She suggested I get Benny formally diagnosed so that he could get even more sessions than we arranged for that day. Here I drew the line. As soon as she left that number went into the garbage. I was going to get an independent evaluation.

As I relay the story to Jennifer, I see the tension growing in her face. In her eyes I see an empathy that pierces me like a knife. It becomes hard for me to look at her. With my own mind, I can play tricks, but I can not hide from the clarity with which she sees my pain. I look and look away as my eyes try in vain to adjust. The sun is flickering through the trees, casting dancing shadows all around. Adam pulls up on the windowsill to see the source of the show, while Benny studies, with great intent, the images flitting across the carpet. Jennifer allows herself to marvel at the boys, and in between her concerns she plays with them. She invents a game with Benny, scampering over the ever changing patterns, getting him to follow, to laugh, and then to lead. I sit back and let myself sink into the soft cushions of the couch. My eyes are full with barely concealed tears, but I also feel a quiet, surprising joy stirring inside. Over the next few months I will learn to let her in and then slowly open myself to others with similar talents.

6 Masestro or Monster

There was a three month wait to see a developmental pediatrician from the leading children's hospital in the area, and in those three months, I read every book on autism I could get my hands on. One night as I sat reading and underlining, my children became friends. Adam would crawl and Benny would chase. Then Benny would throw a ball and Adam would laugh and crawl off to get it. David called me to come watch. I came, my face still tucked in my book, my eyes damp with the tears that had become a staple for me. I did not see what David was seeing. Somehow what I saw made me sad because in some twisted way it made me think of what could never

be. David talked some sense to me that evening and I put down the books and enjoyed my children. Throughout the next few years this became our theme. I worried, I researched, and David never stopped enjoying the children. In the end my work has been enormously helpful, but so has David's commitment to enjoying the moment.

Once I allowed David to open my eyes to the relationship that was developing between our children, I worried a bit less about the future. If Benny at 2½ could be spontaneously playful with his 8 month old brother, I knew that someday he would find his way socially. Still he was not even close to speaking and his frustration was rising.

Jennifer went home but did not forget what she witnessed. She expressed her concerns with each and every phone call. At the same time, Benny was becoming quite unhappy and uncooperative. Judy and Amy introduced us to the term "stimming." Children with Autistic Spectrum Disorders (ASD) tend to engage in repetitive self stimulatory behaviors. They felt that in order to break him of these habits, we had to force him to engage in activities more typical, more social, more growth promoting.

Benny had (and still has) an alphabet bus with twenty-six songs. The bus plays one song for each letter of the alphabet. He also had another musical toy which played many of the same songs. He would coordinate the two toys so that they would play the same song at the same time. He often spent hours with these toys and as they played, lights would flash. Benny enjoyed the flashing lights as well. Periodically his therapists would cover the lights and make note of his rising level of frustration. They told us that we should not allow him to play with these toys. They suggested that he was using them to avoid other contact. We resisted their suggestions at first, but began to feel guilty about allowing Benny to continue to play with them.

The night we hid Benny's music toys in the closet was the first time David cried. I thought at the time reality was beginning to set in, but in retrospect I realize he knew we were doing something terrible to our son. As soon as Benny realized his toys were gone his negative behavior increased. He became angry and oppositional in therapy. He was sad all the time. It seemed as if he knew his therapists were responsible and without language all he could do was rage at them.

I was still taking Benny to a Mommy and Me class at the local Y.

His favorite activity was circle time, when the whole class would sit, play instruments and sing along to familiar tunes. Benny would play happily on a drum or clap cymbals in rhythm. One morning the class was singing Twinkle Little Star. Benny knew this song well and already had picked the correct notes out on his toy piano. I leaned into him and whispered in his ear that maybe he could try to sing along. He began to sob with an inconsolable sadness. His face was red and wet, and he began to gasp for air. I took him out of the class to the lobby. His cry was similar to and different from the cries he let out with his therapists. It held the same anguish but none of the anger. His whole body folded into mine, as he cried for the both of us. He cried not like a child but he cried with the wisdom of an old man. I realized at that moment that he understood everything around him and that he could not sing any more than I could fly myself home. I felt flowing through his body a trust in me that made me shiver. I wondered how his trust could be so strong even as I continued to fail him so terribly.

David and I talked that evening and decided to return his toys. We felt that through his music toys he had found a way to relate to the world. He was learning to listen and processing sounds. He was creating challenges for himself, the same sort of challenges we encourage our students to create. He had taught himself how to grow a bit in a world that must have seemed impossible to navigate. We also decided to terminate his speech therapy sessions with Judy.

We received so much criticism for this move from the social worker, that we decided to find a new agency. I never questioned our decision. It was clear to me that this particular therapy was turning him into a monster. I tried to imagine myself in a room, in a pit, without the ability to move.

In front of me, just out of reach was something I really wanted: a juicy apple, a good book, a CD player with all the great clarinet sonatas, or what I desired most of all—a therapist with genuine insight, who could really help my child. I imagined myself in this position not just once, but every day for weeks and weeks. I thought for a minute about what I might learn from this set up. I would learn to scream and yell and cry. My cries would intensify until I was blue and red in the face and drooling mucus all over my clothes. Then I would look like the monster I was allowing my son to become.

Our appointment came and went with the developmental pediatrician. She was reassuring to a degree but left many questions unanswered. She felt she could not give Benny a diagnosis just yet. She felt he was not retarded, but could not rule for sure on the question of mild autism. In any case her prognosis seemed a bit brighter than the one painted by the social worker. Somehow, despite her Harvard Medical School Diploma, I did not quite trust her. The impact of the social worker's diagnoses, because first and given with more confidence, still took center stage in my mind. I could not reconcile the two opinions and could not dismiss the first.

Our developmental pediatrician did not have any suggestions as to how we could find a new speech therapist for Benny. I called every speech therapist I could find, through our pediatrician, through David's work, and through friends of friends. We found finally Donna, who had worked for a friend of a friend of ours. She was booked solid, but came to meet Benny. She had a nice voice, she incorporated some movement and song in her time with him, and in the end agreed to squeeze him in for three of the five sessions he was entitled to. We accepted and she began to work with him. The first few weeks were very nice. She took her time getting to know him and they formed a bond of sorts. Once she decided to get serious, the problems returned. As soon as Benny realized she was there to get him to talk he rebelled. She brought chocolate and pretzels and held them above his head urging him to say "Ch" or "Pr", but he did not. One night she brought a steamy cheesy pizza which sat congealing on our table as Benny sobbed his horrific sobs while she towered over him saying "Pu, Pu." I could see a change in her. While she greeted him at first with warmth each day now she seemed a little impatient. Her comments to me, while at first were positive, became charged with more concern. As she became frustrated with him, she tried to cover herself by suggesting that he had a disorder more serious than she could address.

I came across the work of Stanley Greenspan, a psychiatrist who works with children who have ASD. I read several of his books which gave me a good overview of his theraputic approach called Floortime. He suggests an approach much different than the ones employed by Benny's therapists. Rather than banning certain stimulatory activities, he suggests joining in with them and ever so gently broadening them. His idea is that if a child is perseverating and you try to stop it, you are initiating a negative interaction. Rather, he suggests that you begin to do the activity with your child and then playfully introduce an obstacle or an opportunity to take a turn. Slowly, slowly you entice the child to react hopefully in a positive way. At the same time you challenge them to add a level of creativity to their play. He breaks down success into such small bites that you can feel successful early on, and allow your child to develop at his own pace. Then you build, always with enthusiasm, always with kindness. It made perfect sense to me. Benny was a child with some social issues. He did not seek people spontaneously as frequently as his peers. He pulled away more when he was upset or frustrated. I tried Floortime and saw immediate results. His approach enabled us to feel good. It enabled Benny to play with his music toys again, and helped us broaden his play schemes. Instead of taking away his music toys, I tried to join. While first pushed aside, soon he was allowing me to take a turn. Within a few weeks of Floortime, Benny, still without words, was handing us recorders and guitars and inviting us to play along as his toys sang together.

7 Spring Shower

Small and waif-like, Mary came into our home with the chilly breezes of early spring. She was the psychologist sent by our new agency to evaluate Benny for his transition into preschool.

She called after dinner one evening and administered the first part of a social history. Within minutes I heard in her voice an intelligence and sensitivity that I knew would take us to a better place. I explained that our son was regressing and his therapists assumed it was the progression of the "disorder."

I admitted that I had accepted that I was most likely in denial, but that deep down I thought he could do better. We were worn thin with balancing the needs of Adam, now almost a year, with those of Benny, a toddler demanding more and more attention. Still, we knew that despite his increasingly difficult behavior, Benny was still a sensitve and delicious child inside.

As we spoke I told her some of what I had been hearing. I shared with her the pessimistic prognoses, and his failure to progress. Still her voice was light and she asked so openly how he was at home, with his new little brother, and how we were managing with him. She asked us with curiosity as if she did not know what the answer would be. I paused, "He is delightful,"

I said. "He is good to his brother, he is kind to us." I remembered how just that afternoon as I sat crying on the bed he came to me, gave me a hug, and looked right into my eyes, as if to say he was there for me. She listened and suggested that perhaps he was in a better place than everyone was reporting. "Even devoted mothers do not often find such joy in truly unmanageable children," she said. That night I slept peacefully for the first time in weeks.

She came the next morning and easily pried him from his obsession with the answering machine. They went to work on the Stanford-Binet at the kitchen table. I sat outside the kitchen. I heard a lot of clanking of blocks, some grunting, and many gentle words from Mary. There was no protest, none of the crying I had become so accustomed to hearing while he worked with some of his therapists. Mary was the first evaluator who showed genuine interest in Benny. Rather than simply tally his incorrect responses she probed and she played. She varied the conditions; she was interested in why Benny could not respond correctly. By responding to his difficulties with creativity and sensitivity, she involved him in a meaningful interaction. She gained his trust and was able to see a side of him that eluded many others. As a result, she saw a child who could learn, who was excited by the possibility of being understood.

After the testing she came to speak with us. Careful with her words, she knew even good news so radically different from the assumptions we had been working with can be unsettling. She let us know she believed his therapists were operating under an incorrect assumption. "He wants to talk," she told us. "He is aware of his limitations and it is devastating to him," she suggested. She thought we should find a new team of therapists. She felt that they were using behavioral strategies to coax him to speak rather than targeting the motor planning issues at the root of his difficulties.

She felt Benny would benefit from both a more holistic approach as well as therapy targeted to help him learn how to use his facial muscles. She did not promise us an easy future. She felt he needed intensive work and a center based self-contained class for the fall. She suggested we concentrate on the physical issues surrounding the control he had over his body, and that the social piece would come as he learned how to use his muscles.

I could not contain myself the next day when Amy arrived. I was bursting inside with joy that a professional had seen promise in my son.

"The psychologist thought Benny had intelligence," I told her. "She thinks that he wants to talk but can't." I explained how Mary varied some tasks and found he had an understanding of many items. I told Amy that Mary did not think Benny was retarded. I could see a discomfort in her eyes as I spoke, my own cheeks filling with blood, both from anger and embarrassment. Amy plowed into her session with Benny and did not say much until Donna arrived for a back to back session. Amy invited me to tell Donna about Benny's evaluation. I did and though they had never met before they bonded immediately. They fell in step with each other and together trampled on the tiny sprigs of hope that had begun to take root in my heart. They spoke in concert, one breaking in as the other paused. There were no silences, just relentless commentary from one to the other.

"She altered the questions?" Donna asked with disdain.

"Have you ever heard of such unethical behavior?" Amy asked Donna.

"No, never, she had no right to tamper with the test, I am shocked," said Donna.

Then turning to me she added: "Diane, you must call the agency immediately and get another psychologist to come in and evaluate."

I tried to explain that she did not count those questions, that she just wanted to see what was going on in Benny's head, but they were resolute. The fact that Mary found anything other than the fog they found in his head was proof enough for them that she was incompetent.

"Diane, we know Benny better," pleaded Amy.

"He needs a very restrictive setting next year and he needs an honest evaluation in order to get that," whined Donna.

With pity and anger, Amy, added "Come on, Diane, you know the truth."

"If Benny wanted to communicate he would have made up hundreds of gestures by now," added Donna.

"He needs realistic expectations," said someone, my eyes and ears closing up at this point.

They went on like this for the duration of Donna's session. Lightheaded, I collapsed on the couch, my two boys plastered on me holding me together as if they knew I was about to crumble. Adam, fourteen months old, began to nurse, and Benny settled into his spot on my right side with my hair twirled around his thumb. Donna came close and in one more act of invasion told me that while it was okay for Adam to nurse, Benny's behavior was unacceptable at his age. Finally, they left, together their voices filled with new-found friendship as they walked to the elevator together.

I sat frozen for several hours. The sun set, David came home and I huddled with my boys until I knew what I was going to do. Much as I despised Amy and Donna, part of me shivered with the thought that they might be right. I realized though that in eight months of intensive therapy, Benny had made no progress. He was especially remote with his therapists who expected very little of him. He seemed much more engaged with family and friends who still saw him as an intelligent quirky child with promise. He deserved a chance to work with professionals who had higher expectations for him, even if in the end he would fail. In retrospect I see now that Amy and Donna failed as therapists, but they were adamant that the failure was Benny's. They had one type of approach and held to it with the rigidity common to the disorders they were trying to treat. They accepted his regression without questioning their own approach. It is alarming to realize how their own failure to help him became their proof of his progressing disability. I chose Mary, but not with the confidence she or I deserved.

I was upset with both Amy and Donna. I considered breaking our ties with both of them, but Benny enjoyed his sessions with Amy. I knew that in general Amy would keep quiet, preferring to scurry out of the house with a few minutes left to grab a donut, than to linger. I knew that I could not allow Donna to continue to work with Benny. After considerable debate about what to say, David suggested I tell the truth. I called Donna and told her that I did not like the tone of the discussion. I explained how uncomfortable I would feel to have her in my home again. I told her that her expectations of Benny were too low. She tried to tell me that she understood how hard it was to accept things sometimes, and then with tears clogging my throat I told her that even if I was in denial, I would have a lifetime to come to terms with Benny's disabilities. For today and tonight and the next few months I was going to lean towards optimism. To do that, I said, I had to choose those who offered me hope. I got off the telephone and for a few moments felt like I could fly.

8 True Sunshine

A few days later Benny had his occupational therapy evaluation. It was a Sunday and I was so drained that I took Adam to a friend's house while the evaluation was in progress. I came home with Adam toward the end to find Benny delightfully engaged with the evaluator, Miriam. He was laughing, pointing, and responding in ways I had never seen before. She liked him, too, and stayed well past the necessary time. She suggested a program of sensory therapy and gave us a list of things to do with him. She showed us how bouncing and spinning caused him to be more related. He made more eye contact and was able to engage in reciprocal play. She was so knowledgeable that I asked her about schools for the following year. She brightened and told us that she worked at a preschool called Little Garden. She suggested that maybe Benny could go there. Little Garden was one of the schools I had hoped we could consider. It was an integrated preschool with fairly high functioning students. Amy and Donna had both told me that Little Garden was too high functioning for Benny. Still in my heart I wanted him somewhere he could grow. I saw a light in Benny's eyes as he played with Miriam and the thought that she felt this school was a possibility for him gave me the confidence to call the assistant director the next morning.

That is how I came to have my first conversation with Diane. With most administrators I was guarded with my words, trying always to get more information than I gave. With Diane, I could not be guarded. Something in her opened me up immediately and I found myself telling her everything. I had already become defensive, altering my description of Benny depending on my audience. With Diane, I was not. From the first conversation I had no compulsion to filter my words. In fact, I could not. I spoke freely for the first time in months. Still, to this day, whenever I speak to Diane I learn about myself.

I remember looking at the angled shadow of the window on the rug, nervously walking it with my toes and trying to stop myself from saying so much. She was, even then, able to disentangle my own projected worries from the reality of Benny's issues. I was a mess, a mix of terror and hope. One minute I saw such potential in him and the next such disability. She let me float in both worlds and gleaned the truth from each.

She explained the procedure: there was first a parent tour, then a child interview and then if all went well she would review the written evaluations. She explained the importance of each step and explained why they could not accommodate all disabilities. She went on to mention that even in cases when a child seems to fit in beautifully at the interview a detail may pop up in the paperwork that makes it clear the fit would not be right. Even as she told me these facts in a most professional tone I could hear warmth beneath reaching out.

In that first conversation with Diane, I began to find my sense of self. She let me talk about the issues, my concerns, and also my hopes for the future. While everyone else heard contradictions, she heard balance. While others accused me of denying the issues, Diane respected me for believing in my child. She conveyed this respect not with words, but with a certain quality to her silence.

We went to meet Diane for a tour. It was a bright and cheerful school. The teachers were buoyant, the students eager. We had visited a few other schools for children with needs and many of them had a sadness in the air. At Little Garden I felt happy, excited, the way a parent deserves to feel when her child is about to begin school.

She took my husband and me to see several classrooms. There were integrated classrooms where children with special needs were combined with children without. There were also self-contained classrooms for children in need of more support. I had hoped that Benny could be in an integrated classroom, but I knew that the group was too large. The self-contained classrooms had a smaller teacher student ratio, and they seemed calmer, less stimulating. Without any commentary from us, she offered to tentatively save him a place in a half day self-contained classroom. I asked her why she chose that class. She looked at me and explained that it was the only classroom where David and I seemed comfortable. In my heart I wanted him in an integrated setting, but I knew that here at Little Garden even in the self-contained classrooms, Benny would be surrounded by children who were much more verbal than he was. I was delighted at the prospect of placing him with children from whom he could learn.

Little Garden, Diane explained, is a school that does not have a time out room. It is a place where severe behavioral problems can not be addressed. I knew Benny could be difficult when frustrated or in a setting not conducive to his growth. I remembered the fits he had with the first team of therapists. I wondered if that constituted a behavioral problem. He had only a few sessions with his new team, but he had been so far completely cooperative.

I was willing to bet that at Little Garden he would be happy, and I knew if he was happy he would be lovely.

Benny's interview consisted in placing him in his "future" class for ½ an hour. Benny was himself, a little tentative, somewhat wide-eyed, somewhat detached, and a little moody. We came during music and snack, his favorites. I prepared him a bowl of strawberries and he ate them happily while the other children snacked on round vanilla wafers. I remember glancing over at Diane. She wore an administrative suit, and sat in a toddler's chair, with her chin resting in her hands. There was a tension in her and a sadness, too. She was completely focused on Benny, and I wanted him in her care.

At the end of the visit, David took Benny outside. He had a meltdown right in front of the school. Within sight of this meltdown, I stood with Diane at a table a few feet from the entrance. I pulled several folders filled to capacity with copies of Benny's evaluations from my backpack. Diane reached out and scooped them into her arms with ease. As their weight shifted into her I heard her voice, feathery, light, and floating freely. It settled softly in my ears. "He is in," I heard her say.

Though unexpected and said in a whisper, there was no doubt about what had just occurred. Her words opened my world. Had she waited a day or even a week, to read the reports, she would have done her job well. She followed her heart instead, and she gave me a gift. She did not want me to walk away with a yearning in my heart or a tension in my soul. I walked out of the school with a happiness that made me skip like a child.

The few months before Benny began Little Garden were pivotal. On Mary's suggestion, the new agency sent us a speech therapist trained in a technique called PROMPT. Prompt is an acronym for "prompts for restructuring oral- muscular phonetic targets." It is a tactile-kinesthetic approach that involves touch cues to the individual's articulators (jaw, tongue, lips) to manually guide them through the targeted word, phrase or sentence.

I spoke with Shelly by phone first. I liked her right away. She was open, friendly, and had an immediate rapport with Benny. During the first session with Shelly, Benny began to talk. She manipulated his face, pushing and pulling his chubby cheeks as if they were soft dough. He let her do it all and this way she taught his muscles how to say ball, then car, and cup and by the next week he had fifty words. He was delighted, excited, amazed with himself.

Shelly was excited, too. She was so excited that she asked to use Benny as her case study for her certificate. She tried a few times to videotape him. She hid the video camera on a high shelf, but each time it she brought it Benny refused to talk. We realized whether or not he saw the camera, she was different when it was there. She was just a bit too eager for him to respond. She found another case study, and Benny continued to make rapid progress. After a few months he did not even need the facial manipulation in order to learn new words. He began to repeat easily and even use words he had heard in the past. Instead of humming he began to sing, and our musical evenings were now enhanced by his voice. Sometimes he would try to sing and play the piano. He knew the words to all the songs he had been listening to. Shelly was very thrilled. I still do not know if it was PROMPT or Shelly herself that helped Benny break through. Until Shelly all of Benny's therapists assumed he could talk but did not want to. They were trying to entice him to speak by withholding a prize until he uttered an appropriate sound. Benny was becoing more and more frustrated.

I knew that he wanted to talk, and that they were adding to his frustration level by holding out objects and food that he desired. Part of the philosophy behind PROMPT is that the child wants to talk but can't. The facial manipulations that the therapists do are designed to help the child learn how to produce certain sounds. The therapist who embraces it has a very different approach than the others. It is an approach I have found Benny needs. He needs support without pressure. He needs high expectations with a lot of comfort. Shelly was only with us for a few months, but in those months we saw that Benny could learn. His outbursts waned; he began to laugh again. He was starting to communicate with the world.

9 Quartet – A Little Music Played Outside

Little Garden was located just a bit too far from my home for me to take Benny myself every day. Eventually he took a little school bus, but for the first few days, I took him myself.

I was ecstatic that Benny was accepted but a little apprehensive when the first day came. He went into class happily and I sat outside on the front steps, with several books to read if I found myself calm enough to do so. There was little time to read that first day, because one after the other, his therapists came out to talk to me.

Miriam came first. She was as full of warmth as I remembered. With great exuberance she told me that she would be working with Benny all year. She told me that she requested him since she felt they already had a relationship. She added that she hoped I did not mind. She stood there smiling at me with a smile that creates instantaneous joy.

Karen came out next and introduced herself as Benny's speech therapist. She told me with excitement that she had just taken the first part of a PROMPT training course, and would be completing her training within the next few months. She said she did it to prepare for Benny. She asked me to tell her more about him, what he likes to do, what makes him laugh. We sat together on the front steps like colleagues embarking on a mission together.

Next came Diane to tell me that Benny was happily eating his snack and I should go for a walk. There was nowhere I wanted to go and so I sat.

A bit later Rena, his assistant teacher, came by just to say that she saw Benny loved cars, and they had lots of cars.

I was in heaven. Three days later Benny was taking the bus back and forth gleefully.

Miriam had a special connection with Benny from the start. Day after day I would ask him questions about school and he would stare blankly back, except for when I mentioned Miriam. Then his whole face would light up. She knew how to reach him. Whenever I visited I tried to catch her session with him. With her, he was animated and engaged. She taught me how to reach that level with him. It was clear that she truly enjoyed him. She did not try to change him. She embraced his quirks and respected his interests. Her approach was very much like the Floortime model we were using with him at home.

One week Benny became obsessed with scotch tape. All he wanted to do was rip it off the dispenser and fiddle with it. She did not stop him, instead she created an activity around it. She had him make scotch tape balls, and then toss them onto targets. Through moments like these they developed a bond that went beyond the routine therapeutic relationship. When his verbal skills began to grow, she would be the first to know. By the end of the first year he would tell her little things about home and school. She would surprise everyone with the information he entrusted first to her.

Benny also enjoyed Karen, and worked very hard in session with her. She, too, let him lead. When he expressed interest in learning the names of the other therapists, she took him around the school. Within days Benny impressed her by learning the names of every teacher in the building. When he was fixated on the phone, she allowed him to call another speech therapist. When the speech therapist had a student, he called the secretary. Once in a while I even received a call from him during the day.

Rena soon adored Benny as well. By coincidence she knew Jennifer's mother. Jennifer's mother did not know about Benny's issues. When they realized their common connection, over lunch one afternoon, Rena described Benny with such enthusiasm that Jennifer's mother called me up to congratulate me on my genius child.

Diane worked hard to make sure Benny's teachers and therapists kept in close contact. While every student was discussed in a meeting twice a year, Benny was discussed every week. Diane knew Benny was more related in therapy and she wanted his teachers to hear it, to learn how to connect with him so that he would begin to relate to them as well.

Whenever I came to the school, it seemed Miriam, Karen, Diane, and Rena were dancing around him. I felt sometimes as if he were the only student there. Perhaps the truth was he needed the most support, but they made it seem to everyone that they were hanging out with him because he was their best friend.

10 Ella

For the first few days after Benny transitioned into Little Garden, I would walk outside with Adam in hand and feel as if I were seeing the world for the first time after a long illness. The trees were greener than I remembered, the sky more expansive than I recalled. Adam was there, by my side, having grown somehow into a toddler, and I finally had a little time to get to know him. I knew that he did not get the attention he deserved those first few years. Those mornings were ours, and we stomped in leaves, ate bagels, and ran through the park.

Adam brought me into the world of the regular neighborhood parent. He ran right in there with the other kids and I was forced to make small talk with their mothers. The world of the regular parent was a new one for me. Parents spoke about expected milestones, sippy cups, and potties. I tried to participate, but somehow the weightier issues were still circulating inside, and I felt even then a distance that would not close.

Raising a child with special needs can be isolating. While other mothers were chatting in the park, I was often prying Benny out of some inappropriate situation. Until very recently he did not naturally follow the pack of children his age, and so I was physically separated most of the time from other parents. After a while I was grateful. With all the pressures inherent in parenting and then the added complications of a daily regimen of therapies, I was just as happy to be left alone. So left alone I was, until I discovered the world of the special needs parent. In this world Benny's behaviors were well tolerated and I had parents to talk with who shared my new language. Although I had survived a lifetime without jumping into groups, I was feeling very lonely. In the past it had taken me years to let a new friend in. Once a friend, they remained a friend across all sorts of circumstances. As a result I have a network spanning decades. They are my family. Suddenly, even some of my oldest friends, friends from childhood, with whom I could always be myself, suddenly made me uncomfortable. I felt a pressure to explain, justify, and apologize for Benny's actions. I felt myself groping for explanations that eluded even the best of doctors. I became hypersensitive to comments meant in the most benign ways. I began to fall away from them in small but significant ways.

My difficulties with my old friends were most pronounced with those who had children around the same age as mine. I guess I expected them to grow together, to be able to play the same way, and the disparity was painful. I wanted to be able to promise my friends that Benny would outgrow his quirks, but I could not. I felt that by continuing to put my children with theirs I was creating an unbalanced equation.

Life in my new world had problems, too. These parents did not all have qualities I desired in friends, and we were bound only by our common issue. With some of them, this issue became the focus of our friendship. One new friend began to introduce me as "Diane, whose son also has special needs." Once I heard those words on repeated occasions I realized it was time to move on.

As Adam played with his peers I sat by and watched the clouds, letting my mind rest for the first time in months. Then I met Ella. Ella's son Matt had been playing chase with Adam for a few weeks before Ella and I exchanged words. Ella was different than the other parents. She had two older children so she was not so interested in speaking about the many milestones associated with toddlerhood. She was eager to talk about education, music, and politics. She was someone I would have become friends with even if we did not both belong to the same equivalence class of parents. Once we began to talk, playground was a whole new adventure for me. I brought extra cars and extra snacks, and our mornings stretched as long as we could make them. Adam loved playing with Matt, and I enjoyed getting to know Ella.

After a few weeks of conversation she hinted about having us all over to her apartment, including Benny. I froze a bit inside. I had mentioned Benny, but I had not mentioned his issues. I was having too good a time pretending to be like everybody else. All of a sudden I felt like I had misrepresented my family. I felt guilty, I felt as though I had a secret life. I was afraid of bringing him into this relationship.

In my mind I imagined pulling away, but I could not. So I told Ella everything. She never flinched in her warmth, never questioned the friendship. Ella embraced Benny fully when they met. And with Ella, from the start Benny was always happy, and with her older girls, he was charming, and somehow Benny became a bit of a role model for Matt, who has no older brothers but only older sisters.

Her acceptance was a real turning point for me. She was a new friend; she did not have to support me. I felt somehow that my friends from the past did not have as easy an out. I questioned their acceptance constantly, and as I questioned I began to erode some of the trust that binds friends together.

Over the course of the year, relationships blossomed between Ella's children and mine, and I realized that some of the issues I had with other friends stemmed from my own perceptions. I had defined myself by Benny's issues and sought comfort in a world where he was also defined by them. In the world of the special needs family, Benny's behavior while accepted was also often labeled. Benny has a fascination with wheels. He often drops to the ground in order to closely examine a stroller or bicycle wheel. To a parent with a child on the spectrum this is a self-stimulatory behavior. When Ella first noticed Benny on his knees, eyes up close to a wheel, she pronounced him a child likely to become an engineer. Over the years I realized Benny is extremely sensitive to how he is perceived. When Ella speaks about how observant Benny is, he looks up at her with bright and clear eyes. He reacts, and he relates, and he is just a bit more engaged with the world.

If not for Adam I am not sure I would have found my way back to the larger world, and I may not have seen that Benny could flourish in this world. I found through Ella and her family that his issues don't have to vanish in order for him to learn and grow from others. Even more important, I learned that Benny can be a valuable influence on a typical child. I should have seen this in my own home, watching Benny and Adam interact every day, but I did not.

I worked to reinstate some of the friendships I almost lost, and I pulled back from the friendships I was trying to cultivate for reasons not intrinsic to friendship. I was beginning to be able to give Benny the experiences he needed with all types of children.

11 Dear Dr. Bigman

Thank you for taking the time to meet with my family last week. Unfortunately we decided not to pursue a relationship with you for several reasons. Though you came to us highly recommended, your performance fell short for several reasons:

While you greeted my speech delayed 4 year old son with initial warmth you very quickly buried your head in his file as you fired in his direction vague and disjointed questions: "Where do you go to school, what color is the truck you are holding, what color is an apple?" While you were evaluating him for proper eye contact you repeatedly failed to look at him, your eyes glued to his thick pile of previous evaluations. These evaluations had been in your possession for a month already.

You went to find my son Lego's when he indicated a desire to play with them. As soon as he became engaged you asked us to put them away so that you could administer parts of a test your associate gave to him little over a year ago. My son objected and with my request you allowed him to play a few more minutes. "Is that a castle?" you asked as he added blocks to his structure. Without waiting for a response you went back to his files. Perhaps you might have noticed in the files that my son did very well on the test you were about to give him, but alas you did not.

After successfully prying my son from his Lego project, a complex project involving many colors and sizes, you administered parts of this very same test. You asked him to place a very large triangle, square and circle in three spaces both upside down and right side up. You were careful to remind us "not to coach."

Did you notice, Doctor, that when my son was "preoccupied," as you wrote in the margin of your score card, with the clock, that he displayed great motor planning and intelligence in dragging a chair across the room so that he could reach the wall clock and that he carefully took it off the wall to see it close up? Did you notice, Doctor, how carefully my son placed it back on the wall without protest when you asked him to do so? Maybe you might have asked him what time it was or what time he eats dinner or goes to school or bed, but perhaps contextual questions would be too easy and might mask the mental retardation you were able to diagnose after only thirty minutes with my son.

In any case, we thank you for your time and concern that the Speech Impaired label my son carries might open him up to frustration if expectations of him are too high. Furthermore, we appreciate your foresight and pessimism in predicting the behavior problems that are likely to develop as this frustration sets in.

Best wishes for your continued success,

Diane Linder

12 Music as a Cure

While Benny enjoyed his first year at Little Garden and had made much subtle progress, I was concerned about the development of his language skills. We had been taking him regularly to his developmental pediatrician who was content with his progress. When I pushed her about my concerns she suggested that I was overestimating his abilities. Consultations with other specialists resulted in similar suggestions. I was told repeatedly that I had to accept his limitations.

I realized that many of the doctors seemed to feel that their job was done when they managed to squeeze his issues into a label. They made minimal attempts to look for ways to help Benny overcome his difficulties.

As Benny became somewhat verbal, I was able to make some observations that I felt were interesting, and possibly held clues to his difficulties. I noticed that he often picked up the tune to a new song immediately and would hum the tune correctly, but he could not reproduce the words. For months he sang the following song to us: "Was da wudda wout toway." I could not figure out what the song was about until he brought me a book on the weather to look at as he sang. I then realized that the words of the song were: "What's the weather out today?" I saw the fog lift from his eyes as I repeated the words again and again. He repeated them with me, correctly for the first time ever. As his eyes cleared they filled with light, and reached out to mine with the intensity of a great and passionate speaker.

Reports from therapists in school praised his focus in therapy and his eagerness to learn. At the same time reports from his classroom teachers suggested he was withdrawn, removed, and unrelated. He almost never spoke in class. While he was speaking more at home, his speech was clearly labored. I noticed that he seemed to use the same words over and over, but always in context. His speech therapist, Karen, noticed that when Benny was asked a question, she would often have to wait up to a minute for an answer. When he answered he tended to use familiar words, sometimes words that did not quite fit, but were related. It seemed as if he was having difficulty processing words that were not very familiar. His ability to reproduce tunes and even pick them out on our piano made me feel that this was not a problem of hearing, but one of processing.

I searched the internet and the shelves of books at the local college library, hoping for direction. I came across the term Auditory Processing Disorder (APD), and immediately ordered several books on it. APD refers to a disorder involving the way speech is processed. People with this disorder have normal hearing, but have difficulty understanding speech in situation where there is background noise. I was not sure Benny had it exactly but I felt that there might be something there that could help explain his difficulties. Over the internet I found many remedies, most very expensive, some very time consuming. It was a new arena for many and somewhat unchartered. There were people claiming to have solutions, miracle cures and the like. Most of the pediatricians I consulted with said Benny was too young to be evaluated for APD, but I read a few articles suggesting that indeed an evaluation could be done at his age. When I ran this by Benny's therapists, they agreed that there was something going on with Benny that we had not yet identified. His speech therapist, Karen, was particularly interested and encouraged me to pursue the possibility.

One evening, I e-mailed several audiologists around the country and the one I was already most impressed with was the first to write back. Dr. Fineman sent me a message the very next morning and invited me to call him anytime.

He asked me many questions and did agree that Benny should be evaluated. He gave me the names of a few evaluators in New York, and suggested I call them first, since he was out of state. He gave me names of people who could conduct the evaluation and then send him the data. He would then make the final diagnoses. I spoke to several of his contacts, but the more I spoke with Dr. Fineman the more I wanted him to see Benny himself. I was worried about the possible subtleties that might get lost between Benny's actual performance and the data delivered to Dr. Fineman. In any case this was to be an expensive evaluation, with no insurance reimbursement and I wanted to have it done correctly.

When I first suggested we make the trip to see Dr. Fineman, David was reluctant. He pointed to our dwindling savings account, the retirement funds we had already used, and the fact that we were still living on essentially one income. I suggested that this could be a trip for my birthday, my 40th, and then he had no choice. I knew someday the fact that I generally refuse presents would pay off. So we made our plans, reserved a hotel, and four tickets on an Amtrak train.

A week before our trip I began to get nervous. I hadn't told Dr. Fineman that Benny carried a possible diagnoses of ASD and Mental Retardation. Perhaps if I did he would have told me to stay home, that those conditions lead to an illusion of APD, but are really something else, something not really treatable, something I would have to learn to live with. Dr. Bigman had told me that he felt this trip was a waste of time and money. He suggested I was trying to escape from labels I did not like. Today, with all these years behind me, I would respond that I was simply searching for ways to help Benny overcome some of the obstacles in his path. I would tell Dr. Bigman that frustration was setting in because my son wanted to communicate but could not. Instead I was silent, for fear of looking more foolish than I felt I already looked.

I thought of calling Dr. Fineman several times, but each time I refrained. I did not want him to tell me to stay home; I sensed that he would point us in the right direction.

I had a dream a few days before we left. Here it is as described in my journal:

Passed Benny in a big castle like house in a neighborhood near to our apartment. Saw him in the window sucking thumb and spacey. I did not have the keys to the house and I ran all over town to find them, to grandma's house, to my house, anxious to free him. I kept passing by this big beautiful house again and again as I ran around town, with Benny motionless in the window, staring and sucking. The keys were nowhere to be found. Could this be my hope that this trip would free him?

Two days later, we left on an Amtrak train. Benny sat at the window and stared for most of the trip. He had a vacant look in his eye that I found particularly depressing that day. We made a few plans with friends. To protect myself from advertising my potential disappointment I told a few people that the trip was mainly social. We spent Saturday and Sunday with Jennifer and Ken. We also met an old college friend of mine and one of David's. Benny was at his best in the hands of Ken and Jennifer and I had a chance to catch up. Now she felt that I was handling the situation well.

Monday morning was the evaluation day, and I was trembling inside. Though Benny had been through many, this was the first I felt had the potential to help. The others were designed to label, to box in for me his prognosis. The evaluation began with an audiological exam and the room had some equipment unfamiliar to Benny. He was scared, he sensed the importance of the evaluation to me, and I could see that his body was frozen with tension. He walked right into the office, lay down on the floor, and began to roll. My face was red with shame. I knew there were no words which could peel him off that floor. I sat beside him, helpless on the carpet.

In a flash Dr. Fineman came in, shook my hand, and lay right down next to Benny and together they rolled and rolled. They rolled until Benny began to giggle and then slowly they got up and Dr. Fineman eased him into the chair and taught him whatever he needed to know in order to be tested. And Benny followed every step. From this evaluation we found out some very useful things.

Benny tested like a hearing impaired child on the regular hearing test with beeps and bells. However, on the section designed to diagnose an APD, Benny was able to recognize every familiar word at every decibel level with all sorts of interfering sounds. Yet he was unresponsive to unfamiliar words at any level of sound. This explained why Benny was not taking in novel words in everyday settings. He was able to learn them only under special conditions, like therapy. Although he was progressing, he was not tuned in to everyday speech and therefore his language skills were developing at a very slow rate. Since Benny could understand speech even in the presence of distractions, Benny did not have APD. Nevertheless this evaluation pinned down for us one of the major impediments to his ability to learn. Dr. Fineman commented on Benny's commendable ability to understand the tasks he needed to do in order to be tested. Off the record, Dr. Fineman suggested that Benny was far from retarded. He predicted that with the right combination of therapies, Benny's language skills would begin to emerge. He suggested a continuation of intensive occupational therapy, and speech therapy with an emphasis on listening as well as producing or repeating words.

Dr. Fineman also recommended a program of therapeutic listening and put us in touch with Deirdre, a speech therapist from Long Island. She was trained in the use of music to enhance listening and to "wake up" parts of the brain that for some are a little underutilized. Therapeutic listening comes out of the Tomatis Method. Dr. Tomatis was a French ear nose and throat specialist. He was one of the first people to study sound and music therapy. He viewed listening as an active, not a passive activity and found that people have their own unique listening styles. He traced many behavioral and learning problems to issues in the way the ear processes sound. He worked on methods to retrain the ear and the brain. These methods involve listening to music that has been doctored a bit in order to engage all parts of the brain. The program Dr. Fineman recommended used classical compositions as a base. Benny would have to wear special headphones which would encourage both sides of his brain to work together. The compositions are altered slightly. Certain frequencies are deleted or enhanced, forcing the brain to fill in the gaps. Dr. Fineman described it as exercise for the brain.

As a classical music lover, I was initially concerned with the utilitarian use of an art form meant to be for pleasure. I disliked the idea of masterpieces altered in anyway. I had always shunned compilation recordings, ones that took famous first movements and put them altogether for those who could only tolerate the openings of great symphonies. I was a purist. I liked my music straight from the composer's head. At the same time, I knew that Benny would listen. I was ready to give it a try.

By the time we were on the train home, just hours after the evaluation with Dr. Fineman, Benny had changed. David slept, and Adam slept. Benny and I stayed awake together. Benny watched the world go by and he watched with an intent I had not seen in him before. He watched with the drive of a boy who knew that soon things would make more sense. He sat with the confidence of a child who knew that finally there was a doctor who believed he could grow.

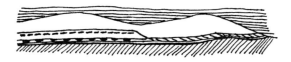

Over the phone Deirdre struck me as a somewhat eccentric passionate educator with great expertise. She would use Dr. Fineman's evaluation as a guide but also wanted me to come in for a consultation in person.

I took the train out to her Long Island office which was located in the town to which we eventually moved. I spoke with her for a full hour. She circulated in and around her CD collection like a chemist handling her compounds. She pointed to CDs for concentration, CDs for relaxation. She had some for writing, and others for reading. It seemed in her world all activities could be enhanced with a little music played at the right moment.

Deep down I was still a little dubious, but Deirdre carried me away with her excitement, and by the time I left I felt a little bit like dancing.

She explained the program Benny was to follow. I bought from her a set of eight CDs. These were the powerful, potent agents that were to help his brain to listen to a broader spectrum of sound. He was to listen fifteen minutes a day for five days in a row. He then got two days off, and would begin the cycle again. He was to listen to each CD twice and then after all eight, we were to repeat. In the meantime, I was instructed to e-mail her every week with his progress. She lent me some extra CDs to fill in with or to use when he seemed to need them. I wondered how I would tell, and she assured me I would know. I wondered if he would sit for all of this listening and she assured me that he would. I questioned what I would write each week as his progress was so slow, for so long now we had stood on this plateau. She smiled a smile I thought only existed in fairy tales.

And so off I went to the train station, and I took my backpack heavy with new equipment home. That night Benny started his listening. Deirdre had told me to begin with two minutes, but Benny would not stop. He did all fifteen and asked for more. Within a week he showed me a squirrel in a tree and had me listen to its chirp. He found it funny that it sounded so similar to yet also so different from a bird.

At home we saw an immediate change. He still was very subdued at school, but he was becoming more talkative at home. There was still considerable concern at school. He rarely spoke in class, and I suspected that his teachers did not quite believe me when I described to them the sorts of sentences he was able to produce at home. I made a videotape to bring to parent teacher conferences. I wanted them to know what to aim for in their interactions with him. I wanted them to know what he could do. We sat at the conferences at a rectangular table. The teachers and therapists were on one side, and David and I were on the other. Diane sat back at the head of the table, a bridge between us, there to help us understand each other, to find common goals, and to be a source of comfort, at a meeting that she sensed might be difficult for me. When I pulled out the videotape, before I even had a chance to turn it on, Diane knew what was coming. On the outside she was professional, and she sat calmly back. For a split second I caught an openness in her eyes, which let me into the celebration taking place inside of her head. If she could have, she would have jumped into the air and let out a cheer. Instead we exchanged subtle smiles, foreshadowing all of the smiles of friendship we were to share in the future. Together we watched faces fill with amazement as Benny's teachers heard him speak with clarity and direction for the very first time.

13 She Heard the Music

The first year Benny spent at Little Garden gave me a vacation, an island of relaxation after and before a difficult time. From day one I trusted Diane to advocate for him as I would. That does not mean I was without worries. Diane invited me to call her as often as I wanted to and I did. I called the first day, and the second day just to see how he was. I called when I feared he ate too many cookies. I called when I needed extra copies of reports. I called when his teacher rubbed me the wrong way. I called when his bus was late. I called to the point when I should have become extremely irritating to her, but that never happened. Instead she answered every concern with care. She called me back within minutes, she followed up our conversations with calls, and she called back at night if she could not reach me by day. For one year plus all my concerns were small. My questions were anxious and compulsive questions, questions that could have been addressed by a secretary. Each time I dialed I felt I should leave her time free for the important issues, the real work behind running a school, yet each week something drew me to the phone and I called. I held back at times. After a few months I decided to keep a list and call only once I had four items to discuss. I told her this, so she would know I was trying to be efficient. Occasionally I would fudge the fourth just to allow myself the call. She sensed this, I am sure. I needed those conversations, and she knew it.

While I was focusing on the trivial, I knew that Diane had her eye on the bigger issues. I knew there was concern at school. He was receiving more therapies than virtually any other student, yet he was still very remote. "In his own world," I was told. Teachers wondered what, if anything, he was taking in. I saw that he got on the bus every day with a skip in his step and that was enough for me. He was happier than ever before and in his whole little body I could see a confidence growing. Diane was not waiting for Benny to produce. She accepted the soft signs that I saw as justification that he was in the right place. She downplayed the tests which showed him consistently three years below age level. She allowed him to "be" without pressure to produce, and she encouraged his teachers to do the same. She allowed herself to marvel at his concentration in therapy, his increasing interest in the antics of his more active peers, and his interest in learning the names of every school staff member. She took all of these milestones as proof that he was growing even though in today's world of assessments and standards they mean little. For Benny, her approach meant everything.

Diane made no promises to me about his future, but she kept saying to me "do not rule anything out." I never even considered the negative of this comment. I always knew she meant it in the positive. I coasted on her grounded optimism for a year. I continued to pepper her with the little things until mid fall of his second year. By mid fall the weight of his future crashed down on me. He was still presenting with many delays. The breakthrough I was expecting for a year had not happened. The upcoming winter would bring a new evaluation for kindergarten, and I knew this would shape his future in many ways. Somewhat disappointed with Benny's developmental pediatrician, I was able to wheedle an appointment with an expert who had a waiting list of two years. I was impressed with myself for doing this, and the high I was on made the fall even greater when we finally met. Mr. Bigman made room in his schedule late on a Friday afternoon. After just a few minutes, he turned to me and said that what he saw in front of him was a retarded little boy, whose parents were pushing him too far. His suggestion put me in a state of confusion. I was concerned not simply because the news was not good, but because I really did not expect to hear that diagnoses again at this point. Benny was flourishing with the early academics in preschool. His speech was still labored, his interests were a little odd, but he loved letters and books, and he could already count. Still I could not dismiss this man, at least initially. He had a fabulous reputation, he made a space for us in his very busy schedule, and though he was removed, he seemed a little bit kind. So I tried again to accept it, tried even this time to celebrate it. Something did not fit, yet I felt remiss to discount it. On Sunday evening, I called some friends and told them. I called friends who were pediatricians, and friends who were social workers, and of course Jennifer. We researched the diagnoses and its implications over the internet together. We tried to wrap our minds around it; we even tried to laugh about it. I was moving towards acceptance, I told myself. I was strong.

On Monday morning I called Diane. This time I did not have four well thought-out questions by my side. Her voice, full with the purest form of compassion, flowed through me and revealed to us both all of the fears I had so carefully buried. Within moments I was in tears. My strength the night before was a show, and in reality I was falling apart. I was terrified about what this meant for his future. I was mad at myself for discounting this diagnosis earlier. I was sure that she and the entire staff of the school knew of my denial. I wondered why they let me get away with it for so long. Somehow she was able to calm me without smothering my concern. She did not tell me everything was fine, but she gave me hope. She did not give me an answer but she gave me the confidence to trust my own instincts.

This was the first of many tearful calls the second year and she took them with the same grace as she took the trivial issues the first year. For the entire year prior she let me express my fears as I could, with clusters of ridiculous concerns. She did not judge me for calling her over a cookie or a pair of wet pants. She heard the music under my words. She took what I could express and built with it a relationship where I could ultimately confide in her fears I could barely admit to myself.

Now I no longer worried I was taking her time with trivia, but I did fear I was taking too much of her time. I saw that she really cared. She cared so much that to step away would have been more difficult than to give. And so I let her give. As she gave, I grew. After a relatively easy life I had to learn how to fall to pieces, how to reach out, and ultimately how to move forward. I was a reluctant student at first, but she gave me time, and in the end I was able to learn. I am not sure there is anyone else I could have learned these lessons from, while keeping my dignity so intact.

As I reflect over the events of the last few years I realize that Diane did for me exactly what she did for Benny. She took him where he was, she accepted him, she cherished him, and she waited until he was ready to grow. She did not expect him to reach any benchmark, she did not need him to pass any test, and she just needed him to be who he could be at the time. She took me also where I was, formed a relationship, filled me with acceptance and support, and gave me the confidence to move on. She knew instinctively that we both needed that kind of environment in order to grow. The world she shaped for us was so nurturing and delightfully comfortable that I knew that I had to find it again. By the time Benny graduated I was ready to move mountains to do so.

And how did his time at Little Garden end? By the last few weeks of summer camp he had a burst of language. He had discovered the power of words and became intoxicated by it. He stayed up until 1 A.M. one night working his magic. A drum became a cake, a pencil the candle. His bed was a slide and his blanket a swing. He discovered pretend play. He became deliriously happy. He began to look for children to play with in the park. It was summer and the sprinklers were on at school. His teacher called me one day to tell me he ran through them hand in hand with a little girl. I was so happy that they could see this. They poured so much into him without any expectations. In the last few weeks they had the chance to see what was inside and they were ecstatic.

At graduation he walked across the stage when his name was called. He paused as they all did for pictures, but instead of focusing on our camera, he scanned the crowd. In his smile there was pride, in his eyes you could see that he was aware of the challenges ahead. He was almost crying but not quite. I looked at his face, and then I found Diane's. She wore the same expression.

On the last day of summer camp I called Diane out of a meeting to say goodbye. We stood together in the same entrance where she accepted my son two and one half years earlier. I handed her a letter written over a period of four months. I needed her to know how much I appreciated all she had done. I wanted her to see how inspiring she had been, and I hoped that she would realize how grateful I was to get to know her above and beyond all the advice she had given to me. She took my letter sealed tight in a light blue envelope. She looked at me and read the contents written also in the lines of my face. She reached for a post-it and wrote her reply. She handed it to me. On the post-it was her home phone number. I promised her I would call, and I did.

14 Yearning

There were so many dreams I had for Benny. I would lie awake at night and imagine him speaking to me, sharing full and complex thoughts. I imagined him as a doctor, years down the line, operating on the very evaluators who continue to underestimate him today. I would watch him on his knees watching a wheel turn, and picture him playing chase with the pack of children who ran by him, falling over with laughter as they dashed in and around the jungle gym. I yearned to see him fully engaged with the world, and I felt it was time to begin to give him that chance.

Music was his greatest love. He enjoyed listening to a recording I had of German Leider. He would listen to it again and again, and while he listened he very softly hummed to himself. His vocalizations began to harmonize with those on the recording.

I found a Saturday morning music program at the college where I taught. They had a chorus for 4-7 year old children. I thought that if he began when he was young, any atypical behavior might be attributed in part to his age. I knew that his skills as a musician exceeded the expected levels for his age. I hoped that this would surface quickly in the class, and take attention off his potential for unusual behavior.

The chorus director was a young exuberant woman named Gina. She welcomed Benny with an open heart. There were nine other children. They were all quiet and well behaved. Benny was not. At the first rehearsal he rolled himself under the piano. He kicked his feet and drummed his hands. I told Gina we would not be back. I apologized for the disturbance. She looked at me and told me that she thought he should come back. She seemed already to know that he loved music. In the midst of all the chaos did she hear that his stomps fell on the beat, and that his thumps fell on the micro beat? Did she hear that his goofy vocalizations blended well with every song? She gave Benny a high five and wished him a good week. She asked Benny if he had a good time, and Benny said yes. I asked Benny if he wanted to come again and Benny said he did.

When the next rehearsal came around I felt a sort of embarrassment creeping up on me. I felt reluctant to face the other parents whose children were on task. I was sure they would resent me, question my parenting and my judgment. Something told me, though, that I had to give Benny this chance to find his way in a group of his peers. When I happened to glance over to one of the other parents, I was met with a kind eye, and that is all. Either they did not notice or they did not care, or they cared enough to give it time. After three months or so Benny began slowly to participate, and by then the other parents celebrated with us. His achievements became a source of joy for them. I suspect this attitude came from the top. Gina set the tone. She accepted Benny, and she wanted Benny to succeed. His success became a goal for the entire group. This was the beginning of my education about inclusion. Benny was not a "problem," he was part of a community, a team, a small little world and this community became a support network for him.

While Benny was in class I often wandered the halls, chasing Adam, and enjoying the ambience of the school. For the first time in years I heard instrumental sounds all around. I heard brass players working on long tones, pianists warming up their fingers with flashy scales, and violinists preparing famous excerpts. The sounds bounced in and around the atrium in the center, and filled me with yearning for the days when my own clarinet contributed loopy lines to the mix of sounds around. In the hallways I met a few former musical colleagues. With each, conversation was similar. These talented folks, like myself, had not played for a while, yet they were up early every Saturday hoping that their children would take pleasure in a pastime they no longer found time to pursue.

It had been years since I had played. The second pregnancy, coupled with the difficulties I had finding help for Benny, allowed days to turn to months, and all of a sudden my clarinet was in a dusty box beneath the bed. I had to play again, and I had to play well. With just a few minutes a day every day, I began to recover my tone. Within a few weeks I looked forward to the ten or so minutes I allotted to my practice. Benny became so excited that we had to buy him a plastic clarinet He impressed us all by his ability to produce a clear and rich sound.

Benny's chorus concert came, and though he knew the words, he did not want to perform. We stayed for the show anyway and he listened with great care. I hoped that by the next concert he might be up there with his peers.

Just days later we were on the subway together, and a girl got on with her parents. She wore a dancer's skirt and she twirled and twirled as she hung on the pole between us. She was sweaty and her makeup had run. She was deliriously happy. She had just performed. I watched her, conscious of a sadness creeping into my heart. I wanted to perform again, and I realized that with all my responsibilities, I might not ever have the chance again.

We got off the train at the next station and I left David and the boys on a bench as I went into the local health food market.

In the market I met an older gentleman. As we each looked at the organic cereals, we began to chat. He told me that he arranged musical evenings once a month in our neighborhood. I cannot recall how or why he came to tell me this, but with the sight of the girl still vivid in my mind, I asked him if I could play. Without the girl still twirling about in my head, I might have stood and offered a silent nod. Since becoming a parent, a certain silence had begun to envelope my more vibrant and exuberant self. This girl reminded me of someone I had been, and this man was there ready to give me a chance to go back. He wrote my number on a box of cereal. He called me the next week, and I had a date the following month to play in the neighborhood festival.

A neighborhood mother, who took a strong interest in Benny, became a friend of mine. She had mentioned that she used to play the piano. I wondered to myself if she and I could play together one day. We were both so busy, it seemed almost irresponsible to ask, and so I was quiet. With this concert date looming, I got up my courage and asked her if she would accompany me. She agreed.

We rehearsed a few times and played in the show. Benny came, listened, and clapped. By the next chorus concert he was ready to perform. We helped each other. He brought me back to a place I was longing to be, and once I was there, I gave him a nudge toward a place he wanted to go.

By the third chorus concert, Benny had a solo. He was still a child who rarely spoke outside the house, and who seemed extremely distressed when asked any question, routine or otherwise. The concert was in a large hall. He did not sing the first three songs. He did not sing the first three verses of the song in which he had a solo. There was a tension in the air. Everyone in that hall wanted Benny to be comfortable; we all wanted him to be happy. I would have scooped him off the stage if I thought that would be best, but I did not. I sat and waited with everyone else. When his solo came, he stepped out in front of the group, and he sang. His voice filled the entire concert hall with a sound both soft and sweet. There is a dance between every performer and his audience. This was a dance with great tenderness.

I had tried to thank Gina many times for her patience with Benny, but I never seemed to find the right words. I always used ones that she did not accept. Words like "challenging" and "difficult" were not in her vocabulary. She would reject even more benign ones like "typical" and "mainstream." After the concert I went up to her and I used only the words that I had heard the other parents use. To Gina I said, "Thank you for a wonderful concert." It seemed that I finally found the words she could accept.

15 Spring Fugue for Three Voices

Spring 2007 came in with the challenge of placing Benny in a kinder-garten class for the fall. The first whiff came in a December phone call from a district psychologist named Laura. She impressed me with her down-to-earth and friendly demeanor. Within minutes we discovered that we were colleagues at the local college where we both taught. David had already informed the district of our intent to have Benny evaluated privately. The district still needed to appoint a psychologist to be present at the Individualized Education Planning (IEP) meeting and they chose Laura in the hopes that we would feel comfortable enough with her to allow her to do the testing. She was both intelligent and personable enough to allow me to trust her, but in the end we did have Benny tested privately. The district only provided for a verbal test of intelligence. Since Benny still had significant verbal delays, I was concerned that a verbal test would not have been a valid measure of his cognitive abilities. Nevertheless Laura was responsible for observations of Benny, interviews of his teachers, and incorporating the results of the nonverbal IQ test into a cohesive report. She was also charged with choosing a "label" for Benny and recommending a placement for the fall. The "label" was to be chosen from a list of thirteen recognized by the state for educational purposes.

Laura proved to be as competent throughout the process as she was in that first conversation. She called me often, filled me in on her thoughts, was honest about her doubts, and frank about her feeling that he fell between several diagnostic labels. She worked hard to find the best one, speaking, on several occasions, for an hour or more, to Benny's preschool teachers. She even made a few calls, in vain, to Albany to try to get permission to use a label that was not on the list. My own conversations with her were intense and often strained, but I always knew she was listening.

Benny's IEP meeting came in early March. I came prepared with books about special education law. Prior to the meeting, I had introduced myself to professors in the department of special education at the college where I taught. Over the course of a few weeks, I read every book those professors recommended.

In the course of my brief study of special education law, I came across the Individuals with Disabilities in Education Act (IDEA). This law, first enacted in 1975, gave disabled students the right to a free and appropriate education. It also contained many guiding principles. A student must be educated in a general education classroom to the maximum extent possible. A child should only be removed if education can not occur in satisfactory manner with the use of aids and services. A child may not be removed for convenience. Special education, I read, is a service and not a place to which student is sent. The principle that stood out in my mind was that a child with a disability is entitled to accommodations, aides, and services, if he needs them in order to function in a general education environment. If a child cannot function in a general education environment for all subjects, then the team is supposed to consider each subject individually and indicate precisely why the child cannot function with typical children in that area.

They must try to find a way to support the child with his typical peers. The team must work to place the child in the Least Restrictive Environment (LRE) affording the child maximum contact with typical peers. I knew Benny could function with typical peers in music, gym, and art and I wanted him to have that experience in school.

Each district is required to have a range of options for special education students. The range of services available to students is where each school system differs. More specifically, the systems differ in the texture of their options. Some offer discrete class configurations. Others offer a more flexible array of services, which can be tailored to the child's needs.

As I debated possible placement options with Laura I saw that we were approaching Benny's placement from very different perspectives. She knew the city well, and saw him as a child who needed more support than was customarily provided in a neighborhood school. She came trying to place Benny in a spot where he would be most similar to his peers. I came with the conviction that he could function with his typical peers and with the confidence that he could learn. I wanted Benny placed in a setting where he could grow. I felt empowered by the words of the IDEA and privileged that I had them to bring with me to our meeting.

Laura first suggested we consider placement in the special education district, which would mean he would take a bus each day to a school outside our neighborhood. The schools in this district are primarily for special education students. A few are housed in buildings that also house regular classrooms, but from what I had seen, contact between special education students and general education students was very minimal. Placement in that type of setting would have made even casual interaction with typical students difficult if not impossible. As a result this was not an option I was willing to consider. I accepted the need for a special class, for the academic subjects, but wanted him with his peers for specials. Laura agreed to place Benny in a self-contained 12-1-1 class. Since discussion began with the suggestion of placement in the special education district, this appeared to be by comparison a less restrictive setting, and in her view was the LRE in which he could function. This was a class that was housed in select neighborhood schools.

When I explained my intention to have Benny attend music, gym, art and library with a general education class, there was a shift in the dynamic, a silent sigh, a sense that this would be a longer meeting than expected. Laura explained to us that if Benny were to be "mainstreamed" for specials, he would be taken to the door by an aide and left there, on his own, with the new class. I knew this was too much to ask of any five year old, and certainly one with transition issues. I was irritated initially. In front of me I had this chapter paraphrasing the IDEA. I looked at my book and read the passages over and over first to myself and then to the group. Laura explained again and again how things would play out in our city. I knew she cared, she had spent hours on the phone with me, but momentarily I was upset with her. Suddenly I remembered Jennifer's frustrations, as she traveled the country working to gain accommodations for workers covered by the 1990 Americans with Disabilities Act (ADA). These words in the IDEA, as well as the ADA, are subject to interpretation. The interpretation can be challenged but then it becomes a legal issue. I realized I lived in a city which did not interpret these words as I would have liked. I knew a legal battle was not something I wanted to confront.

In the end, I would not leave until we stipulated that Benny would attend music and gym in a general education setting. Laura knew that no school would honor this part of the IEP, but she agreed to it. Laura shook her head as she wrote up the notes. On her face was a mixture of respect and pity. I walked home not quite knowing how to feel. I liked Laura and I trusted Laura, but I did not like what she was trying to tell me. I had no idea what was in store for us. Laura did.

In March, just weeks after our IEP meeting, Nancy came to town. In all of the years we corresponded we had not spoken. It is eerie that she came to my city right as these decisions were being made for my son.

She was presenting at a three day conference and left an entire half day free for me. We met in the early morning at the Tramway Café, on 60th and 2nd, across from the hospital where I was born. Though it had been almost twelve years since we spoke conversation came easily. She had not changed much, still a passionate gentleness in her eyes, and an insatiable interest in people. I felt that I had changed more, aged more at least inside. I had crossed over to her world, although she still came with more experience.

We spoke about music and children, and reminisced. Adam was with us and we took him to the Central Park Zoo. She had fun with him. After the Zoo, Adam fell asleep and Nancy began to question me about our plans.

She came with the knowledge that I had just agreed to a fairly restrictive placement for Benny. From my perspective I had fought hard to keep him in our local school. I would not leave the meeting until we found a way to have him mainstreamed for part of the day. While I was able to have this written on his IEP, I knew in practice it would be a challenge. Nevertheless I was proud that I got it on the IEP, and I felt I scaled a mountain to have him placed in our very own local school. For Nancy this was nothing. She knew that separation from his peers even by a classroom wall was too much.

She asked me repeatedly if I really felt he would be better off separated. I fumbled around. I tried to justify it. I suggested it was temporary, that by second grade maybe he would be mainstreamed. She knew I was trying to be positive. She explained how acceptance becomes more difficult as the children age. She pointed out the quirkiness of five year olds, and told me how they naturally take care of each other. She suggested that friends he made now would stand by him as they grew together. While I mentioned the benefit of learning to read in a smaller class, she focused on his need to learn social skills, and conversational skills. She told me more about her son, and how much he grew from his interactions in school. She offered to come to an IEP meeting with me. She often attended them in the Midwest and explained how as soon as the officials saw her, they knew that inclusion was going to be the result. I knew that she underestimated the constraints here in my city, but I could not find a way to explain it.

As we talked and as I shared pictures and stories, she became more and more concerned. She knew we were making a mistake. We walked fifty blocks or more, and she continued to ask questions and offer suggestions. I tried to listen, I tried to understand, but I did not. I sensed a gloom rising in the space between us where there was once laughter and music. I told myself it was a mistake to let a piece of Apple Hill into reality. She walked me not only to the train station, not only to the platform, but onto my train. She did not give up, though the flow of conversation had been reduced to a trickle. She stood outside the window until the train pulled out. We stared at each other like parting lovers who have so much more to say, but can't find the words or the time or the wisdom. I rode home with great sorrow and could not say why.

I sat with Diane one morning in late April as we poured over school placement options for Benny. The district gave us a choice of schools in the area. There were pros and cons to each of the choices. Diane questioned and listened and questioned again and in the end pulled out from me my best guess as to which situation would work. No sooner had the words left her mouth she sighed and offered this remark to me: "Well, we can not know for sure if this is the right fit, but I do know that if it is not...you will make it work...somehow." Wrapped up in this remark was so much. That comment left me dizzy each time I replayed it in my head. Until that moment, all the corrections and adjustments had been carried out by her. She used my instincts as her guide but she did all the work. Her comment that day was both compliment and command. It contained a transfer of power from her to me. She knew there would be difficulties ahead, but she felt I could overcome them. It was an honor that she had such faith in me and at the same time, it was terrifying to realize that she would no longer be in charge. I tried to begin to channel my anxieties into something productive. If I was going to have to take charge I needed to understand what made Little Garden such a positive experience for all of us. I began to write. Each night after everyone was tucked in, I reflected. Out of these reflections came the beginnings of this book as well as a few very grateful letters of thanks to the staff of Little Garden. These evenings kept me calm, reminded me of the growth that was possible, and fed my determination to find another place like it.

Between spring and fall these three voices, those of Laura, Diane, and Nancy, circulated within me. On the outside I was unchanged, unmoved, plodding steadily on the course I set up in early March, but inside beneath the level where even I could sense, I was changing.

From the IEP meeting on, Laura provided a steady beat, not always what my ear wanted to hear, but a necessary part of the story. She told me with great clarity and sincerity what the city would and would not be able to do. She knew what I wanted but knew all too well the constraints. I then came to value her for her ability to see the problems in the system and continue to do her best to help those that had no other options. Her answers became more predictable as my knowledge of the system grew, but to hear the reality of what the city could provide was a necessary part of our journey.

Nancy's disappointment ran through me for months like a soft stream cutting its way through rock, changing it, sculpting it, with almost silent motion. Nancy alerted me to inclusion and with passion told me it was the only way to go. Though I shut her out initially, her story stayed within me. While I made excuses to myself at first, I continued to feel her eyes upon me, questioning me, begging me, shaming me.

At the same time, over these very unsettling times, Diane's confidence and support channeled through me, soothing, cooling, and smoothing the wounds I incurred while watching my son fall to pieces in the NYC public school system. I did not have to call her every day to hear her voice echo through me. She believed in me with a sort of unconditional confidence that I could accept from her because I believed in her with the very same sort of confidence.

As Benny became more distressed, Laura ran out of options for us. She laid out a few which we tried and admitted that our options were close to exhausted. She was then a bit remorseful, and offered to stay in the loop. Her honesty was valuable and her interest sincere.

I kept going back and reading the excerpt Nancy sent me on inclusion for her son. I saw the obstacles she and her husband scaled; I saw it was not easy for them either. The text centered on his adjustment to kindergarten, but she also sent me a video clip of her son walking across the stage to get his high school diploma with his peers. I could see the wonders she described to me.

Every week or two I would call Diane. Her sadness for us was real but she never lost hope. She knew I would "make it work," and though at the time I had no idea how, I believed her and she was a great source of calm for me.

These voices began pianissimo, singing so softly they were felt and not heard. Through the summer they intensified ever so slightly, a gradual crescendo into late summer. By the time reality dawned in September they sang to me at full voice all day and all night.

16 Kindergarten Song

Mom: "How was school today Benny?"

Benny: "Kevin threw a chair, he did not get a sticker, Ivan threw a chair, he did not get a sticker, I sat like a pretzel and I got a sticker."

Mom: "How did you feel in class when this was going on?"

Benny: "It makes me very upset. Ms G says, 'Ay ya ya I will call your father.' "

Mom: "It must be very hard for you to be there."

Benny: "My school is closed because it is snowing."

Mom: "It is not snowing today, Benny."

Benny: "My school is closed because it is too cold out."

Mom: "You have to go to school."

Benny: "I will go to Gina's school, Gina's school is open, and my school is closed."

Mom: "Gina's school is open only on Saturday."

Benny: "Little Garden is open; I will go to Little Garden."

Mom: "I wish you could, but you graduated preschool last summer."

Benny: "We have to get me a new school."

Mom: "Yes, Benny, we do."

—Morning Conversation, Mid September 2007

Benny wakes up eager to start his new school. We walk down the block alongside our neighbors. I feel like we have scaled a mountain. As I exchange smiles with the other mothers I realize that what is routine, expected for them, is a miracle for me. I am full of gratitude that we can send him to our local school, which is running a self-contained 12-1-1 class, the very type of class the district thought he needed. I feel fortunate because not every school houses this class. Many children with special needs have to ride a big yellow bus each morning, to a school far away.

I am conscious of how far Benny has come in the past two years. While he still presents with numerous delays, he has shown that he can learn. While his behavior is quirky, he is cooperative. He jumps up and down and waves to a child he recognizes from the park. He is beginning to reach out to his peers.

When Benny spots his teacher he runs to her and gives her a hug. She hugs back and takes his hand. They walk in together. She has a light in her eye. I want to believe that we have found our place.

I wait with eagerness at dismissal time alongside these mothers who come with lesser concerns. Some wait with treats or presents. I wait empty handed. I am in a different world than they are. As soon as his teacher approaches I see that the light in her eye has been extinguished. She hands Benny to me and tells me that she had trouble "reaching him" today. She hopes it will be better tomorrow. I see Benny is sad too. Somehow I know already that it will not work. It is my birthday and the first day of the class I teach at the local college. I walk with sorrow down the big bustling boulevard until we meet David. He has a flower for me and somehow that makes me even sadder. He tells me to give it time. I know though the look, the look of a teacher who does not "get" my son. I know no time will solve the problem, because once Benny is not understood he will only slip further away.

Three weeks into the year and now there are other undercurrents as well. One day the teacher tells me she is looking for a book about children with "Benny's condition." I thought a degree in special education prepares teachers with books on all conditions. I wonder what condition she thinks he has, but I do not ask. I am strangely quiet these days. Another day she tells me that Benny is not functioning, which I know are the words I hear before he is moved down. For him this would be to an 8-1-1 class, a class housed in a special school, a school outside the neighborhood, a class without an academic program.

I attend Open School Day, and I promise myself that I will give her some tips on reaching Benny. I will fix the situation, I will help her learn about him and it will all work out. Instead she lectures us about her goals this year, and the homework policy and there is little time for us to talk. In the middle of her presentation a parent comes in anxiously looking for her child's class. She expected to find her name on the list of parents outside the door but it is not there. She wants to know why her name is not there. The teacher tells her that her son has been moved to another class. The mother is confused. Her English is poor. The teacher tells her that her son has been moved to General Ed. She gives her the room number. The mother still does not get it. After a few more unsuccessful attempts to explain the teacher says "Ma'am your son is *too smart* for this class." The mother brightens and goes on her way. I catch a glimpse of my reflection in the window of the door. Peering back at me are sad, hollow eyes. I recognize them as the same eyes my son wears as he makes his way out of the school building each day. They have replaced the sparkling shiny eyes he wore just weeks ago.

I visit the bookstore and I find a book on inclusion written by a professor in Syracuse. I e-mail her in the evening. I also send an e-mail to Nancy. It took a few months for me to hear her words, but tonight the impact of Nancy's mission last March comes to me fully. She invites me to call her immediately. She is ready for me, relieved that I heard her, and happy to help. She gives me the names of a few districts around the country that are inclusive. The closest she knows of is in the mid-west. I do not care; I am ready to move to the moon in order to place Benny in a regular classroom.

Over the weekend I tell David my plans. He has all the arguments of practicality. He has to finish the school year, we have no money, and our parents, who are a great source of support to us, live here. I pretend to listen and consider these items but inside I am determined.

Monday morning I realize that I have not spoken to Diane in almost a month. I have thought of her often but tried to resist dragging her into my crisis. I do not want to use her only for advice and support. I need to hear her voice, and I want to be in touch. I know we need to have a different relationship now. Although she handed me her home phone number on Benny's last day of preschool, I am not yet ready to call her at home. Instead I call her at school, at the number I have dialed so many times. I try to engage with her in a regular conversation. It works. I ask her about her life and we discover that she grew up in David's hometown. They even attended the same temple for a while. She tells me a little about her children. She asks me about my music and I invite her to a concert I will be giving soon. I do tell her things are a little up and down at school for Benny. I try to play it down; I tell her I am working on it. I ask her if inclusion works. She tells me it does if it is done right. I suggest to her that I am interested in finding an inclusive district for Benny someday. I mention Syracuse. She shivers from the thought of the cold and from the distance and the upheaval for our family. I play it down though, just a thought I tell her. She tells me she will come to my next concert.

The next day I pick Benny up at school and he stands pale with his teacher. She is red with anger. She tells me she wasted her afternoon trying to get Benny to learn his colors. She tells me she neglected her class to do this and in the end he did not even try. I see that he is shaking and I take him straight home. He has a fever of 103 degrees and I lie beside him in the bed all afternoon and night. I do not sleep. I cry for him with constant steady tears.

In the morning I call his teacher. I tell her that he is sick and I question why she did not notice. I tell her I do not care if he can label yellow but I care that she failed to notice that he was ill. She wonders aloud if she will catch it.

I take out his IEP and read to her the section where he correctly labeled 11/11 colors last spring in preschool. She has an answer, a theory. She informs me that children with "Benny's disability" are rote learners. He learned the colors in preschool and could probably identify them there, but can not carry it over to a new situation. I ask her to have him identify the color of her shoe or her hat and see if he can. She tells me that is not part of the assessment she must complete by October. She tells me he does not know his letters. I suggest that she watch him spell the names of every child in the class with ice cream sticks. She tells me that she would lose her job if she did that.

I realize that I have said all I could say. I hang up and sit paralyzed with sadness and rage on the floor. I can feel all my strength, all my hopes, draining out from me, spreading into the spotted carpet beneath me. For the first time in a long while my mind is blank. The emptiness is almost soothing. For a moment I feel as though I have done all I can, there is nothing left to do. The telephone rings. It is Diane and she does not wait for me to speak; she is too excited. She found the names of four districts on Long Island with some degree of inclusion. She tells me Syracuse is too far; she tells me I should call her more often and in her voice I hear great disappointment. Something greater than the details of her call reaches out to me. This "something" pulls me back to a place where I can function. Her call takes me to a dreamy state. I can not explain by science alone how she knew the extent of my despair, when I disguised it so well. I can not explain the fact that she called at such a low point by coincidence alone. The scientist in me is beginning to believe in magic.

I write down the districts she has for me on a slip of paper. I carry this slip with me for days until it infuses me with the strength I need to make the calls. This slip of paper reminds me that there is someone who really understands.

17 Jennifer, Variation II

As I endured tremendous stress each day here in my little world, Jennifer continued to tackle these enormous issues that touched upon the very same matters that consumed me. It was an interesting confluence, and one which bound us together in a new way after a friendship lasting nearly a lifetime.

Around this time, Jennifer began work with a small team to restore the 1990 Americans with Disabilities Act (ADA). This act was designed to give people with disabilities protection in the workplace and beyond. The ADA presents an obligation to mediate physical impediments to those with disabilities. The implications of that section are straightforward. The section affording protection to those with mental disabilities or physical issues that require more subtle accommodation are trickier. The ADA has been subject to interpretation by the Supreme Court many times, and some folks have been caught in a ridiculous loophole. In order to qualify for protection under the 1990 ADA, one must be substantially limited in a major life activity as a result of their disability. For example, when epileptics are on proper medication, they are not considered disabled enough to be protected under the ADA, according to the Supreme Court interpretation. Therefore, while they can function better than those with uncontrolled epilepsy, they are not able to request job accommodations which would make it possible for them to remain in good shape. There were also gray areas surrounding protection for those with learning disabilities, and sensory processing disabilities.

Jennifer rewrote sections to close these gaps. As she wrote she had to check continually with representatives of various special interest groups to ensure that they could live with the new wording. Some groups, school administrators, for one, were afraid that a tighter ADA would make them responsible for providing more services. Jennifer had to find a balance and it was not easy. As soon as she lightened it to please one group, another group would raise an objection. She was in between many impassioned people and had to live in that space for months. Somehow because of our years of friendship, and also my interest, I became her release. She could call me at any time of day, since I was almost always available, and vent. And I was learning more than I ever imagined I could about legal process, interpretation of legislation, and the power of the Supreme Court in setting precedent.

Jennifer's other interest struck even closer to home. She was involved in a campaign to persuade states to provide a range of services for those with mental illness. The research favors inclusion here too, with positive outcomes for those who are cared for in as natural a setting as possible. There is a tendency for state-run institutions to require in service care in order to qualify for services, when a person with mental illness might be served as well if not better, outside the facility. It was in some sense the same issue we were facing with Benny. It was interesting to hear it play out through Jennifer on a much larger scale. Hearing her stories made me realize that our issues were just small instances of broader systemic ones. I realized that I would not be able to challenge the city and win on a time scale that would have been any benefit to Benny.

In my own life, I could not have felt more self-centered and narrow than during the times I sensed Benny was not in the right setting. I felt some days as if all I did was collect information. I called every contact, took advantage of every connection, and once in a while, when I looked up for air, I felt myself a selfish and driven individual. I had lost some of my ability to connect with others for mutual pleasure. Jennifer gave me a chance to do just that, while maintaining my focus on the issues I could not let go of even for a minute. A call from Jennifer was a peek into the real world, and I could be helpful, just because I could make her laugh. Somehow, my concerns made her feel more connected to the every day ups and downs of life. I think too it helped her to know that someday this work, this very difficult job she had, might just benefit this little boy whom she cared for deeply.

When she called five times in two days to see if I liked the wording of the section she felt was most related to Benny, I wondered what she thought I could contribute. I think I know now. I contributed the interest, the gratitude, and the thrill of being close to a person who had some power, at a time when I was feeling very powerless.

18 Freedom

Each day was heartbreaking. Each hour had a different slant to the pain. I could not tell if the sadness began as Benny cried himself to sleep each night or if it began in the bright and early morning as he plastered himself on the sidewalk as we approached his school. Once he was in school, I lived each day as if walking on shards of glass, knowing that throughout the day, my child was suffering. There was no relief upon pick up, and the evenings seemed to be the worst. In short, the various types of agony tumbled upon each other creating a constant vortex of despair.

One day Benny came home with bite marks on his arm. "Not to worry," I was told when I questioned the school, "he bit himself." We decided that evening that he would not return to that school.

We still did not know what exactly we were going to do. I was ready to move, David was feeling rushed. He kept telling me to slow down, that we could make it work here, that we had to make it work here. I told him that I had given up, but he could try. I felt that this was the first issue that threatened really to divide us. It was as if I was riding a wave that was destined to take me and the children to a better situation. Benny's misery was affecting Adam as well. Adam announced one day that he, too, did not like school. I had no energy to try to convince him otherwise, and for a few days we all stayed home together. It was a vacation for us all. We cuddled, we drew, and we danced. In my home we were safe. I could have kept them there forever. It was one of the possible worlds available to me: my home forever, or a new place, a place where I would not have to fight in order to get my child an education. In either case I knew what it was I desired. I desired peace.

A few weeks earlier over the Jewish New Year, I read an article by David Wolpe in The Jewish Week. The article consisted of a short column suggesting that God gives us ladders and it is up to us to ascend or descend. The visual was immediate and I saw us as a family descending. All the work Diane and her team put into Benny was draining away. He was losing his interest in people. I knew he could make up the academics, but his spark for life was fading fast. I sensed that we had little time.

David made a few phone calls to local administrators and requested that Benny be moved to another local school. This touched off a flurry of attention to him and all of a sudden he was being considered for an experimental program where seats were in great demand.

At 9 P.M., on a Wednesday evening, the phone rang. It was an administrator from our district. She called to tell me that Benny might qualify for a coveted spot in a new "experimental" program. The program held the possibility of a semi-inclusive placement eventually. There were six rounds of evaluations. If he were to pass all six, she explained, he would have a seat in a self-contained class designed for children on the autistic spectrum. In order for them to proceed with the evaluation, we would first have to have his classification changed from Speech Impaired to Autistic. Then he would spend two years in kindergarten. After the intensive two year term in kindergarten, several of the six students would be placed in an integrated first grade class. I cringed from the thought of all the competition involved. It bothered me that children with disabilities have to compete for what ought to be their right.

I questioned why he would have to spend two years in kindergarten, and she explained that intensive work would be done on social skills, and that it would take two years to cover the regular kindergarten material. She told me that experts would be on hand from leading universities to guide the teachers. She explained to me that I was very fortunate to have this opportunity. I asked how many students were competing for this spot and she told me that they were holding it for Benny. I wondered to myself how out of 160,000 special education students in the city, they chose my son.

Momentarily I felt a swell of pride, but soon questions filled my head. I asked her what would come after the two years for the students that did not "make it." "They," she reported, "would go into a self-contained twelve class at the same school." She reassured me that places would be set aside for the students not chosen for inclusion. "Ahha," I thought to myself, "the very same type of class he is in now." I realized there was a difference though; the children that did not "make it" would be essentially left back. Something seemed circular, swirling, dangerous, a sort of gamble I was not willing to take.

The conversation lasted longer than it should have. She wanted very much to convince me that this program was right for Benny, and I wanted very much to believe her. She wanted very much to offer me something that could work. I knew that the program she described was not the right one for Benny, but I could not let go. I could not let go to the public school system that gave me an education, to the city that I had come to adore, or to a system that I felt was in need of all the support it could get. So I hung on to the conversation and so did she. In a turbulent sea we found a space for ourselves where we could breathe. Here we were, strangers, trying to find a solution, well into the night. I hung on to this conversation and so did the administrator. We hung on well past the point, well beyond the time we both knew the truth. We were on the phone until an embarrassingly late hour. My children were sound asleep. David had turned out the light, and my upstairs neighbor had turned off her television. Finally we gave up, with regret on both ends. I fell asleep with the comforting knowledge that someone in my city tried.

Perhaps it was this comfort that gave me the courage to call the districts that Diane gave to me. Maybe it was the sense that there were no reasonable placements available in my city. In either case, it was not easy for me to make the next round of calls. I felt a sort of desperation inside and I did not want that to show. I wanted to sound collected, intelligent, and in control. In reality I felt my world shifting beneath my feet, I felt pulled by forces beyond me, I was completely committed to moving, and in this complete state of commitment, I felt like I had no control.

The next day, I set the boys up with puzzles and videos and sat down to call each district. I had my best pen in hand, and used my important voice. I made three calls this way, and spoke to three administrators who could not make me any promises. They could not say for sure that Benny could be integrated. They would need papers and reports, and evaluations done by their own people. We would have to be in the district before they could even begin the process. The boys soon became hungry and I went to the kitchen to make them omelets. With them at my feet I made the last call. I was sure it did not matter, I had little hope left. What follows is all I remember of the conversation. I remember mainly my words. With the chatter of the boys and the splatter of the eggs, and the shame welling up within me, I could barely hear the supervisor. Yet I knew that we had found a place.

—Hello, my name is Diane Linder. I am a teacher with a child in a self-contained special education class in NYC. I am very unhappy…I feel he needs more opportunities to be with typical peers. An administrator at his preschool suggested I call your district. She told me that you offer some inclusion programs.

—Benny…How do I even begin…He has speech and sensory issues, some autistic features as well. He tests several years below age level, but he can learn. He blossomed in preschool but is quickly losing all his gains. He is picking up a lot of negative behaviors in school.

—Oh, really, you did? Oh so you know…

—Yes, he is falling apart, fast. Do you have any openings?

—Yes, I know inclusion means spots for all, but I just called three other districts and they tell me that there are no guarantees.

—How can we apply?

—You accommodate everyone? Yes, I know that is what inclusion means...

—I know I have to live there.

—Yes, yes, I know real estate is sky high, I have a beautiful apartment here that I will sell.

—I just need to ask, how do I know this will work for my son?

—Yes, I have read some research on inclusion that is why I called.

—Sorry, I am sure you are busy.

—It is just that he has lost so much ground since he began kindergarten. Maybe he will need to repeat a grade. They tell me here he will have to repeat kindergarten.

—You advise keeping a child with agemates?

—Interesting, yes keeping a child with agemates makes sense, especially for the social role models.

—What happens if we move in the middle of the school year?

—You always have a place for a child in the district, really?

—What if it does not work, where does he go?

—How do you know it will work?

—Yes, I trust you, I guess, but I don't even know you. Who am I speaking with anyway?

—Oh the chairperson herself! Oh...sorry to take your time.

—Yes, yes it is your job, and I appreciate your time.

—A real estate agent, yes, yes I need an agent, I know I wish I could move tomorrow.

—I have an apartment to sell too...

—Get him out of that class. I know, I know; it is a disaster.

—Yes, I have thought about home schooling him for a while, but he needs his therapies.

—Thank you, thank you, I appreciate your time. I will call the agent. We will be there before the end of winter.

Next, after I called the agent, I called David at work. I called to tell him that I had made an appointment with a realtor on the weekend. I heard a tension in his voice. He realized I could not hold back. He asked me if I could slow down. He said he felt that it was too soon to look at houses. He wanted to try to make it work here. Gently he suggested that we wait until the summer to look, and that maybe in the meantime we could work things out here. I told him that sometimes the picture is very clear, and that all I saw here was disaster. When our conversation ended David explained the situation to a few of his colleagues who were standing nearby. A colleague he had only a passing acquaintance with happened to overhear. She heard the name of the district in discussion and she handed him a phone number. A former teacher from David's school happened to be married to a retired special education supervisor from the very same district. We called him that evening.

The man spoke with a deep and cheerful voice, weighty enough to demand respect. He gave his time freely. He spoke at length and with pride about the district. David and I strained to listen together, over the clamor of our boys. He was relaxed, and able to explain to us all the details I could not take in on the phone call with the current supervisor. He spoke about the inclusion students in middle and high school. He told us about the children that grow so much in the program, the children that have no limitations placed on what they can learn. David was listening with an intensity I had not seen in him, maybe ever. By the time we finished speaking with this man, we both knew we would be moving soon.

That evening, I became conscious of forces that seemed to be out of my reach. Suddenly it seemed to me that events were unfolding with a synchronicity that went beyond coincidence. I was struck by how dependent I had become on others. I knew that had it not been for Nancy's personal experience with inclusion, Jennifer's expertise with disability issues, Diane's incredible insight, and finally this retired supervisor who fell into our world to give us the final push, we would have been stuck. I had always envisioned myself as a very independent person. I lived my life alongside others, but I did not see myself as one who was affected by others in any substantial way. I remember my joy when I first read Leibniz, in college. He describes a world made up of "monads." These monads are fundamental particles, without parts, and completely self sufficient. Within each monad, a reflection of everything exists. Life unfolds such that everything appears to be related but in fact is unfolding in accordance with a "pre-established harmony." Each soul can be thought of as a monad, "windowless," as he describes it, without being subject to influence by others. He explains how this creates an illusion of a deterministic world, but that in actuality each soul is perfectly independent as far as the influence of other things. This view brought me peace. It explained the beauty of the world and at the same time gave to us complete autonomy. Until recently I was proud of my ability to find my own way, to resist peer pressure, to remain unsusceptible to advertising, to make my own choices in friendship and love. I felt that on some level I had never really been altered deeply by anything outside my body. The world view of Leibniz seemed to account for my experiences in music. Each player works from a score, where his lines are clearly delineated. Each instrument has a part independent from the rest, yet when the parts are heard together the illusion of causality is present. A running scale begins with the flute and passes to the oboe; a thumping bass line intensifies until it appears to cause an explosive recapitulation of the theme, but in actuality these parts are independent, practiced over and over in the isolation of a practice room. To me this was an example of the kind of pre-established harmony Leibniz describes. I became conscious another level of causality. I thought back to Apple Hill and the Spohr, and the summer I spent working on those songs with Nancy. Though the notes, the tempos, and the rhythms had been set ages ago by the composer, the experience of playing these pieces with Nancy was incomparable to any such experience since. She influenced me—she caused me to play the notes a certain way, more mournful here, maybe more hopeful there, as the lilt in her voice led to a response from me, and then back and forth in an endless infinite loop, that shaped those pieces into something incredibly unique and completely original. Her influence was not imperceptible but was and is indescribable. I began to think that I had spent a lifetime overlooking the indescribable. The influence of one musician on the next exists on the level of the felt, not the spoken. I began to worry about how much in the world I had failed to recognize simply because words did not suffice to explain. In the world of music, my beliefs denied the very most profound and human aspect of playing music with another. Somhow, in music, these beliefs did not hamper my performance. Perhaps the nonverbal nature of it or the shear joy of music making carried me past this limited view, and allowed me to connect on a level I would have argued against. In life and friendship I began to suspect that I had been hampered by a certain rigidity that was melting away as I allowed my friends and colleagues to influence me in ways I had never dreamed possible.

All of a sudden, I could not deny the profound influence of my friends any more than I could deny the tremendous influence of Benny's teachers on his development. Leibniz's model suddenly seemed inconsistent.

I felt myself falling back to questions I left behind in my brief study of philosophy I began to explore a little on a piece of paper, and soon I needed a pad. I drew lines here and there, similar to the force fields I drew in physics class. No simple sketch could explain to me how I got to this point. I found myself up late one night trying to understand my designs, trying to decide whether these events really refuted the idea of a soul, my soul, as one impermeable to influence. I had let my friends in, and by letting them in, I ceased to be the person I was for so long. There was a connection present between myself and others that was new, and in the midst of all the tension, this connection brought to me a steady stream of pleasure. This ability to connect, while born in relation to those that helped me the most, did not end with them. I felt it in the supermarket, and I felt it on the bus. I had always been a friendly person, but I was relating to others in a new way. I sensed a vitality that began to charge all of my relationships. Of all the changes that were to ensue over the next few months, this, the least visible, was, to me personally, the most profound.

My mind turned to the other parents of children in Benny's class. I recalled the stony silence with which they would stand at dismissal time. The parents of the typical children would stand in packs and chat. They shared information, compared notes on teachers and policies, and came together as a collective voice. The parents of the chilren with needs were isolated. They did not form connections with each other easily. My own attempts to engage them were met with little encouragement. I promised myself that over the next few weeks, I would reach out to them and begin a conversation.

After a weekend of house hunting, we took Benny to several schools in the inclusive district. New Yorkers by nature, we decided to walk to the schools from the train station. By the time we arrived at our last stop Benny was worn out. He dropped his tired body on the sidewalk and refused to go in. I went in alone. I walked into Mr. R's office and found a room filled with color and light. In front of me were a large round table and a man in a yellow suit with an irrepressible smile on his face. Despite the importance of this day I was at ease. I was honest. Although this man had a tremendous reputation for excellence of every variety, he seemed almost a little nervous. As soon as he began to show off his school, I was able to stop him. "I am not interested in the gym, or the computer room, or the new playground," I said, "I need to know if my son can function here." He put away his smile for a moment and we sat down at the table. "Tell me about your son," he said. I took him to the window and had him strain to see his body crumpled on the sidewalk rolling a car back and forth and forth and back. "There he is," I said, expecting him to send us away, He did not. He grabbed his coat and took me outside. He positioned himself right on the sidewalk next to Benny. He began to talk to him. At first Benny tried to brush him away, but within minutes he was upright, telling him his age, and then introducing his brother. I had not seen Benny so engaged in months. I knew we had come, for now at least, to the end of our journey. In the presence of this man, and the joy I knew he would bring to us, I was no longer worried about my relative freedom. The principal took my hand and said, "This will work, we will make this work."

We went down the block and put a bid on a little cottage.

He made this commitment in the absence of reports, of evaluations, of any kind of testing. Like Diane, he made this commitment from the heart. I wonder what we can take from this as we move deeper and deeper into educational reform driven by assessments. I wonder how important it is to the world that these two people saved my son. How is our assessment driven system serving students who will never perform at capacity? Children like my son, left in the special education system in most districts, are doomed to failure.

While relieved to have a plan, I was filled with insecurity. How did this man know my son could function in inclusion? What if this does not work? David and I asked ourselves these questions every minute, yet as we questioned constantly, we sold our apartment, we took a new mortgage, and we borrowed money for a car. We prepared for a new life in the suburbs. In the meantime I lied to the administrators at Benny's current school. I told them he was going to a more restrictive setting, because that is what they believed he needed. I could not defend my choice yet because inside I was still too afraid. I did not have the words to penetrate the language of the NYC system. How could I begin to justify my hope that he could survive, let alone flourish in a setting alongside typical children? How could I explain my plan to sell an apartment I loved and move to a town I did not, just to give my difficult child a chance? There were no words to explain this. In the absence of words I told lies.

19 Teacher Observation

Teacher Observed: _Ms. K_

Class Observed: _Special Education Kindergarten_

Time of Observation: _9:15- 10:45_

Reason for Observation: _Open School Day- Ms. K suggested I sit beside my son in order to keep him seated, and to witness the difficulty she had "teaching" ever since he arrived. This is Benny's second school of the year, another 12-1-1 class in our neighborhood. Benny has been in the class for two weeks._

Please use the first and major portion of this form to report a descriptive record of the lesson. Please include no evaluative comments. Simply state what took place during the lesson. The final paragraph may include an evaluation of the lesson.

Observation:

At 9: 15 Ms. K gathered all the children to the carpet area, a narrow slip of space wedged between the desk and the first row of tables. She requested that they form a circle, but the space allowed only for an oval of sorts to form. A student was asked to come to the calendar and point out the correct day of the week. He became a bit disoriented and was asked to sit down. Ms. K then went on to finish herself. She pointed to each day of the week and stated both the name of the day as well as the date. Ms. K made no mistakes.

The readers were then distributed. Little booklets made of newsprint paper; three were given to each child. Each book was six pages long; each page had one word and one picture. The titles were: Lunch, Park, and School. Each book was read three times. Considering that each book had six words, the children were exposed to 54 words in all. The children were very familiar with the booklets. They apparently use them every day.

After the nine readings the teacher introduced the terms title author, and illustrator. The title discussion went very well. The children had no problem identifying the titles of each book. These books lack an author and an illustrator, and the teacher tried very hard to define these terms in the absence of an example.

The entire lesson lasted a full 1 ½ hours. Three children had to be removed for disciplinary reasons. My son was chided several times for appearing uninterested. On the whole the class sat very well. They sat for the first half hour, and they sat for the second half hour and they finished up by sitting for the third half hour. The parents were very proud particularly if their child sat well.

All in all, it was good that I was there to help my son sit. If he did not sit the teacher might not have been able to teach. Everyone would have been very disappointed.

20 Thursday

Each day I come to pick up my son at school, the second school of the year, as unsuccessful as the first, and I hear more complaints about my son. Even in another special class for children with disabilities he can not seem to function. I am powerless in the face of these teachers and administrators. Several of them stand together and catch me as soon as I walk in. They point out my son who is running around when he should be sitting. They tell me this is what he is like all day. They tell me that he is frustrated because he has no "kindergarten readiness skills," and that he should not be in an academic setting. Even though they all know that we are moving to another district in three weeks, they let me know that they can barely stand to have him for one more day. The teacher tells me every day that she has had to "stop teaching" ever since Benny arrived in her class. She points out to me students who are regressing as a result of his presence in her class. Each day I must go through this ritual and each day I reply the same way: "Yes, he runs around I see. I see, you just told him not to and there he goes again." I remind them that soon we will be gone, out of their hair. There are no other words available to me, though there is so much more to be said. Instead I take his hand and turn quickly toward the door, the pain hot in my chest as I leave. By the time I reach the far corner of the block the heat spreads out, warming my elbows and my knees. It feels more and more bearable, almost comfortable now as I walk in the coolness. I begin to reprimand him: "You need to listen to your teachers. You must stay in your seat." I ask him why he misbehaves. I ask him what will be in the future if he does not learn to listen. It does not surprise me that he does not give me a verbal answer. He is holding my hand and I am listening with my fingers. There is both kindness and strength in his grip and for a split second I can see the future, and I see that he will be fine. He glances up at me with big brown eyes, and I begin to question myself: "Why do I, a teacher myself, have no impact on his teachers?" "Why do I let them abuse me so?" Then finally, the warmth hits my toes. He begins to sing "Ha'ir Be'afor," a Hebrew song about Paris, A City in Grey, and we pass an older couple who hear him. They smile at us and I feel almost normal again. I open the notebook and I read the notes from his therapists. I see they are still working on material he mastered a year or more ago. That is where he presents and they take him from there. He doesn't protest and he fails to label every color and so they spend more time on these skills. I write them another note back letting them know that he knows this material. They will disregard my words. To them, I am a mother in denial.

On most days I take a slow long walk home with Benny. He does not like the playground anymore. Lately he resists most situations involving other children. When I lure him there with a promise of sorts he spends the time under the equipment counting the metal bolts. So the walk is our activity. I try to give him what I know he needs. I give him some chances to succeed and he takes them with eagerness. I let him take the lead and he tells me what he sees- the cars, the trucks, the birds in the trees. He tells me the letters that begin the words he uses, and then often a few more words which start that way. He is ready for reading, I think, but his teachers do not see this side of him. I tried to show them several times but I could see their minds were set. So we have our plan. It is an odd time now, waiting for something I hope will be better. I enjoy these long afternoons with Benny. Together we say goodbye to the neighborhood I have lived in for forty years.

Thursday is different, though. I work on Thursday evening and so I pass Benny off to his Daddy and get on the bus to become for a moment a teacher of teachers. I am a teacher of teachers who can not make a school situation work for my own son. I am a teacher of teachers who can't engage in a meaningful dialogue with the teachers who matter the most to us. But there I am before long in front of a room full of elementary school teachers looking to me for answers. Recently I have begun to feel lost in the classroom. I used to come to class prepared with a folder full of crisply paced activities. My goal was to create mathematically literate teachers who could divide fractions three ways and turn triangles into hexagons with ease. This semester my goals are changing. My students speak of standards and rubrics and pressures to test. I think of Benny and his teachers and the way that he is evaluated each day. I see how terrible it all is, how their constant judgment of him has created a cycle where he will never be able to succeed. I want to tell them to forget it all. Forget the curriculum, forget the assessments, and just think of the students. Find one student who can't sit, can't seem to focus and reach that one. Abandon the workbooks and readers, take out only books which they and you love and read them again and again and again. Keep searching for activities that capture the most remote child. That is what counts. But instead I try to stay on task, keep to my plan, but it is difficult. Now I hear myself say words like numerator or denominator but as the words come out streams of thought wash over them. I am not even sure what the students are hearing these days. My class lacks focus. Students drift in and out, marking their own papers or fiddling with their phones. I let them as I stand before them trying to work out for myself where I am going. Some nights I come close to telling them about my son, but I resist. I am afraid of where it will lead. I am afraid I will not know when to stop. I am afraid I will cry. I do not have enough distance yet to figure out which parts of my story are relevant. The past few weeks I found myself telling them about previous students of mine who brought varying degrees of challenge into the classroom. These stories work well for me. They touch on the issues I am consumed with and inspire some interesting discussion. It is a different type of teaching than I am used to, but I am beginning to feel comfortable with it.

A few Thursdays ago I told them about Andrew. Andrew was a highly active, somewhat impulsive fifth grader who I taught eight years ago in a selective K-12 private school in NYC. He was a child previous teachers warned others about, a child the administrators would have liked out of the school. There was talk that he would not make it to middle school, his skills were weak, and he had "issues." We were asked to keep "notes" on his antics- a paper trail to nudge him out. One Friday during a geometry lesson Andrew really could not contain himself. He was jumping off his chair, challenging my every word, and creating havoc in my classroom. The other children were feeding off his activity level and the result was near chaos. My first mentor once told me that when a class is out of control, it is best to pretend that you are supportive of it and at least maintain an illusion of control. That was my guiding principle here as I "stopped teaching" and told the class to count all the squares in the room. To my surprise Andrew took the challenge seriously and came to my desk a few minutes later. "I found thirty-five hundred squares," he said. The light in his eye told me we were in for something special, and I followed him to the door. There he pointed out to me as well as to a silent class, the rectangular glass panel inset right above eye level. He stood on his toes and showed us the thin wire embedded in the glass, with seventy wires one way and fifty wires the other, crossing perpendicular to each other to make thirty-five hundred squares in all. In those few minutes, as Andrew spoke, he gained the respect of his peers. I knew then that there was a lot more inside this child than his behavior allowed one to think. I wish I could say I planned this activity but I did not. I stumbled onto it so I could sit down for a few minutes and break a cycle of disruption. Nevertheless, this was a turning point for Andrew and that math class.

I asked my current students to think about why Andrew was successful with that activity, and to consider what other activities might also capture his interest. My students took off with this. Discussion flourished on many levels. Some saw themselves in Andrew, and others saw some of their current students. They came up with all kinds of alternate activities for virtually every topic we had covered this semester. My hope was that they might be inspired to give some of their own students a chance to succeed by design and not wait for chance.

The next Thursday I told them about Pam. Pam was an eighth grader who had failed math for two years before she turned up in my remedial eighth grade class. She was described as spacey, wildly disorganized, with huge gaps in her skills, and in general thought not to be a good fit for the highly rigorous high school ahead of her. I began that year with simple graphing and from the start her graphs were incorrect. Each was incorrect in a different way with no visible pattern to her errors. Her handwriting was so messy that it was difficult to even read her work. Yet she worked with a confidence not often seen in such a weak student. She did not seem to want help and would practically turn her back to cover her work when I walked past. After a few weeks of this I decided to try to get to know her a bit. She wore elaborate jewelry, some of which she made. Her jewelry was very geometric. I asked her about some of it and she brightened. I realized that anyone who could design jewelry with so much mathematics in it must be a mathematician inside. Once I realized this, although I kept it quiet, she let me in. I sat beside her one day during class work and she told me her secret. She used a different scale for each axis of her graphs every time. She put the negatives where the positives go, she went up by a varying amount on each scale, and tried a new variation each time. She said that the graphs come out more interesting that way.

I left the story at this point for my teachers to consider. Again the discussion took off. They were animated, engaged, and stimulated. They figured out quickly what Pam's difficulty was, and they questioned why it took so long to see. There was lively debate on this point with some initial skepticism. They did not want to accept the fact that the school had failed her so badly at first. They looked for ways to blame her. She was defiant, she was disorganized. It took a bit of discussion before one student voiced the possibility that she was shut out by her teachers who made assumptions about her abilities and pushed her away with their harsh judgments. Soon after that comment, many looked into their own past and found times when they were misunderstood as well. Some questioned their own teaching, and wondered about their own judgments, and then I knew we had gotten somewhere. I stopped feeling guilty for neglecting to teach them more about fractions.

On the very same evening that we discussed Pam, a current student of mine, Sara, came up at the end of class. She had a concern. A project was due soon requiring my students to read a picture book to their class. The book I chose was <u>Henry Hikes to Fitchberg</u> by D.B. Johnson. They were to write up the discussion and plan a few activities to advance some mathematical point from the story. Sara said she was worried: "I teach preschool special education," she whispered, as if she were ashamed. She went on to say, "They can't follow this book. It is above their level, and if I read it to them our discussion will be very poor." Furthermore, she explained that she was concerned that her write up would be weak compared to that of her classmates. She wanted permission to read it instead to an on grade level group pulled out from a friend's class. My immediate response was outrage. I wondered where she was these past weeks while we had these glorious conversations about seeing past limitations. All of a sudden it was clear to me that the failure was mine. Here in front of me was a student I did not reach. So at 9:30 P.M. after all my other students left, we stood together in our classroom and I told her about my son. She listened. I told her that my own special needs child likes this book, can discuss it, and even acts it out as we walk around the neighborhood. I told her he relates it to other books we have read although his teachers would never believe me. I told her she must read it with her students and see. She looked right at me. She understood and she said she would try.

The next week the papers were due. My students were engaged, sharing their stories and comparing the discussions their students had on this book. Sara was late, and when she walked in she began to talk with her coat still on, breathless with excitement. Sara took the stage. Her class amazed her. They followed the book. They saw connections she was sure some of us had not. A boy who had never spoken in class participated. She turned page after page of the book and recounted the observations of her students. I invited her to describe her students. They are severely delayed, some on the autistic spectrum, many with trouble focusing, difficulty sitting still. She described them with pride. Surprise filled the room. Young students, students with needs, saw more in these pages than many older abler ones. Sara was speaking straight to all the thoughts in my heart, and everyone in the class was tuned in.

Tonight, just days before our move I check my e-mail and find this note from Sara: "Thank you for everything. I really enjoyed your class and learned a lot. Not only did I learn a lot of content but I learned a lot about my students. I will never underestimate my children again." I read these words and the pain of these months is momentarily gone, washed away in an instant. Fresh like after a dip in a new found pond, I sail, I soar inside. Something in the world has changed. A ripple spreads out from our crisis and spurs growth. I walk into Benny's room and sit by his sleeping side. I read him the note. I tell him the story and he smiles in his sleep. I know now that someday we will find what we are looking for.

21 The Old Man and The Subway

One would expect that when a child with needs is around typical kids his issues will stand out more. I hear this fear often as I talk with other parents, especially those who question me about inclusion. As we prepare for our move, I am confronted daily by parents who want to understand where we are going. While I am still lying to the administration, I cannot lie to these parents. They follow me out of the school and catch me once we are a safe distance away. Every day for a week this happens, each day another parent. I tell them that we are moving to a district where Benny will be in an inclusive classroom. Each parent reacts the same way, with a look of both awe and pity. They are confused and intrigued. The feeling that pierces me the most is the one I struggle with daily. One father articulates it the best. He asks how I will deal with watching my son beside normal children when his behavior is so odd. He reminds me how strange our children look even when alongside other children with issues. In my mind I see his son painting the table with ketchup every day, as Benny hides his head in his elbow and sucks his thumb. I wonder this too, I tell him, but I am ready to try.

There is a period many of us pass through when we want our child to "look normal." We want not to have to explain or apologize. Maybe at some point we give up on the hope for normal and settle for "not so different." Maybe that is the comfort we find in segregated settings.

Shortly after Benny began kindergarten he became fascinated by the subway gratings that line the streets along our main boulevard. Each time we passed the stretch right by the fire house, Benny fell to his knees and stared with fascination into the dark and dirty abyss. I would ask him to stand up, yank him by the arm, and if all else failed, scoop him into my arms and carry him until we were well passed the temptation. He would cry and scream and my arms would ache for days. One day as he fell to the ground, I saw an old man kneeling there as well. He was looking for something, I told myself, and I yanked Benny away.

The next day Benny ran to his spot, and I noticed that the old man was there. I could tell that this man was not looking for anything in particular, but he was looking at something apparently very interesting. I saw a softness in the man and he smiled at us. This time, I did not pull Benny away. Instead I bent down and I looked, too. There had been a recent rain and in the space beneath the grating, the entire boulevard was reflected. When the train passed underneath the reflection shimmered and quivered and Benny laughed. We stayed for a long while, until Benny wanted to move on. Until that day I was waiting for him to grow out of these things. The sight of that man suggested to me that he might not. When I bent down, I saw in the gutter a universe worth exploring.

Suddenly, after that day, I stopped waiting for Benny to be like everyone else. I began to celebrate Benny for his differences and not in spite of them. I think it was a helpful place to come to in order to move ahead with our plans.

I tell the story to the father. He asks some more questions about therapies and services. I explain that Benny will have all the supports he has here but he will be part of a general education class. He asks me to keep in touch, to let him know how it works. His eyes search mine, looking still for an answer. We lock eyes for a bit, our gaze steady for a few moments. I wonder if somehow I am giving him a bit of what he needs, even though I am far from sure myself of anything.

22 Saying Goodbye to My City

As we prepared to sell our two bedroom apartment in my favorite section of New York City, to move to a cottage in what looks to me like nowhere, I began to get very sad. I knew we had to go, and I knew we were not going far, but at times, the idea alone brought me to tears. I thought about the city, and realized that what I would miss most was the way we in the city fall into each other's lives. There is little privacy in this city, and at times there is great comfort to the ease with which we learn from and enjoy each other.

Walking through the neighborhood with a special needs child can be an adventure. A child with differences announces himself without reserve. While once a private person, I was thrust into the limelight as my son began to walk. Maybe in the end this was good for me. Each venture, even to the grocery store, became a prism through which my neighbors passed, the flexible, the rigid, and some very kind people. Through watching their reactions and then my reaction to them, I have learned more than any Master's Degree in education could impress upon me. I saw that the sort of intelligence needed to relate to Benny is not one found in the halls of prestigious medical schools; it is a sensitivity independent of terminology, advanced degrees, and even words themselves. At first it was tough, I saw the disdain, I felt the judgmental eyes of my neighbors burning through my clothes, as I tried often in vain to tame a meltdown.

It did not take me long to find that hidden within many of my fellow New Yorkers, there are riches. First I found just a few, but now I find them all over. Like watching the night sky, at first you see a sprinkling of stars nestled into the blackness, then as your eye adjusts, soon the whole night sky is filled with light. Tonight as we prepare for our move, the whole town is sparkling, and I say goodbye through a curtain of tears.

Benny met Leah when he was three days old. Fresh from the hospital, we stopped in to buy diapers. A month early, born on the first night of our first day in our new neighborhood, we were unprepared. Leah was the cashier in the local "everything store." From pots to creams to crackers and toys, you can find it at this store. As I later learned you can also get counseling, spiritual cleansing, and prophecies for the future, if you catch the fancy of Leah. Benny did.

From day three Leah knew Benny was different. Tucked and swaddled, and fast asleep, she barely had to glance at him to pronounce him a "special child." "A child who will see the world in new ways," she said, straining to find the English words for the Hebrew which came into her mind as soon as she laid eyes on him. Leah bonded with Benny from the start; she got a smile from him as early as the grandmas, and could tame a hunger meltdown faster than I could fish out a bottle. From the first moments Benny could walk, he would walk us right into her store. He would stand before her with perfect eye contact, and smile. Leah and he would laugh together, as the line grew and grew, with, at times impatient customers. Leah would take her time and turn to me to report, "See Diane, the boy is a genius, and listen to what he tells me with his eyes." When we began the cycle of evaluations and therapies I would walk by her station with sadness. She would grab me by the sleeve and whisper to me again and again: "Diane, this boy is all together, I tell you. . .I see it, I know, inside he is fine, the words will come. Look in his eyes, I tell you." When finally the words did come, Benny would run in to share them with Leah; he would run behind the counter, into her arms and whisper something new, and she would flood with happiness though never surprise. Still to this day, we visit her often, and she never forgets to remind me that she always knew.

Benny went through a period of time when he did not like to wear a hat or gloves. This, I have heard, is a period many children pass through, but most can be cajoled, or bargained with, or tempted by a color or character. A child with needs is different here because when she or he decides they really do not want something, they can plaster themselves across a sidewalk in frigid conditions and howl a howl reserved for the monster movies.

One blustery day in January, as I walked Benny home from Mommy and Me along the windiest stretch of our main street, Benny decided it was time to remove his mittens. Adam was still a baby and I was steering a double stroller, in case Benny would sit. It was a day of negative wind chills, a day of frostbite warnings, a day when other toddlers were wrapped in blankets and sealed inside plastic covers on their strollers. Benny wanted no part of any stroller and certainly no plastic and all of a sudden no mittens. My request for him to put them on led to a horrific fit, and as I reached to catch his head before it hit the sidewalk, his mittens blew away.

An old woman was passing in a threadbare coat, with a face etched with kindness. Shivering from the cold, she was walking slowly, painfully, until she ran and lunged for his mittens. She then held them, fluffy, thick, red, and woolly as if they were precious jewels. She reached down to Benny and as she handed them to him, she showed him her gloves, old, tattered, torn. Without words she lifted him up, and helped him put them on. She smiled at me a smile with broken teeth, and when I tried to thank her she touched my hands and walked away. Since that day our paths have crossed many times, and we have shared many warm smiles. Benny has never complained about wearing his mittens again.

All over NYC it seems every block has at least one store which sells miniature versions of vehicles. There are police cars, cabs, city buses, and school buses. Benny had a huge collection but insisted on stopping into at least one store per day. A seasoned collector, he just wanted to look to see if there was one he did not have.

One afternoon it seemed to me that there was nothing new, which was usually the case. Benny picked up a large yellow school bus that played the ABC song when a little black button was depressed on the roof. I knew he had an identical one at home and I reminded him of that. Benny was not listening to me, he was pressing the little black button over and over and he was interested in the fact that this particular bus made no sound. Benny pressed and pressed and the bus did not make a peep. He took it to the register. He told me he had to buy it. I told him we had one just like it. He told me that this one was different. I suggested that he pick out one that worked properly. He looked at me with a look suggestive of my ignorance and said, "I want the one that can not sing." I glanced up at the man behind the register, who has been selling us vehicles for years; we both were aware of the subtle change in the air. I had to finally accept that I had become a parent who has a lot to learn from my child.

Shortly after Benny began to talk he began to sing much of the day. Often he sang softly, but on public buses he sang with more volume. The excitement of the travel, the background hum of the bus, the audience trapped around us fed his enthusiasm and he sang with full and loud voice. Often Adam would join in with his softer, gentler, and younger voice. Most of the time his song was not welcomed. I would sit tense with the knowledge that if I tried to stop him he would meltdown, a meltdown far more disturbing than his song. So I would scan the crowd for friendly faces and finding none would turn my gaze inward.

One afternoon we all boarded the M104 on 102nd Street. It was a long ride to Penn Station and Benny was in good cheer. He began to sing immediately. Adam joined in. Within a few seconds of the ABC song, the bus driver began to sing along. With full grin, with rhythm accompaniment he sang and sang. By 96th Street a few other passengers were humming, by 72nd Street, the entire bus was alive in song. By 59th Street Benny had exhausted all his favorite American songs and switched to Israeli melodies. Those who were familiar with these tunes joined in with even more vigor and those who did not know them began to clap or tap, to keep connected to the music. The bus was crowded now, people hanging on to poles, bodies touching in that way that only seems to happen in big cities, but everyone was happy. Some folks strained to get my attention, to smile, to connect with me, the mother of the boys who sing. Those who could asked me what other languages they speak, where they go to school, and what are they like at home? If I had tried to tell them that one of them had special needs I would not have been heard. To these people on this bus, these were wonder children, and I was a very fortunate woman.

When it was time for us to get off the bus, the music was over for many. We exited to a round of applause, and I was thrilled that I got to go home with the musicians.

These New Yorkers and others like them let me keep my dignity and kept my spirits high even on the darkest days. I will miss my New Yorkers more than I can say.

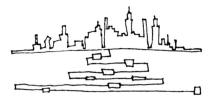

23 Paradise, June 2008

"I am so glad for both of us that this has finally come to an end."
—Special Education AP, NYC, January 2008

"Benny, it was such a pleasure to have you in my class. You have certainly grown, and I know you will shine in first grade."
—Inclusion Teacher, LI, June 2008

Benny: "In September I will go to first grade."

Mom: "Yes, Benny, you will."

Benny: "Where do I go after first grade?"

Mom: "You go to second grade."

Benny: "Oh, and after second grade I go to third grade, and after third grade I go to fourth grade, and then I go to fifth grade."

Mom: "Yes, Benny, you do."

Benny: "Where do I go after fifth grade?"

Mom: "Then you go to middle school."

Benny: "And where do I go after middle school?"

Mom: "Then you go to high school."

Benny: "And where do I go after high school?"

Mom: "Then if you want you go to college."

Benny: "I want to go to college. And where do I go after college?"

Mom: "After college, if you like, you can go to graduate school."

Benny: "I think I want to go to graduate school."

Mom: "Then, Benny, you will go to graduate school."

—Morning Conversation, June 2008

I wish I knew more about why inclusion works. So far I have heard no fancy terms, no specialized language. In these four months the only words I have heard from Mr. R and others at the school are permutations of his promise to me that October day. These words work very well for us. Just last week, Mr. R was in the playground. His eye caught mine, and he ran by and grabbed my hand. Together we looked at Benny playing happily with another child. "I told you we would make this work," he said. That is the essence: they make it work by keeping an eye on each individual child. The child is in the regular class and the goal is to make it work. There is no place for the child to go "down" to in the system. When faced with challenges, the school looks into ways to make things better, with the goal of helping the child to function better in the class he has every right to be in. This way the child moves up always. And it works. Each day there is progress, and each day there is joy. Everyone feels it, the child, the parents, the teachers, and the administrators. It seems so simple now. I write in the hope that somehow, someday my city that lies just 15 miles west can taste some of this joy too.

We have made it work so far, and it is not as though Benny has been easy here. He brought all of his issues with him.

For the first few weeks it looked as though all our problems had evaporated with the move. Benny's new teachers greeted him with such warmth and kindness that he made instantaneous progress in the first few minutes of the first day. They began immediately to teach him and found that he could learn. The other children embraced him both figuratively and literally, and Benny came home knowing all their names by the end of the second day.

After a grace period of a few weeks, Benny began to get comfortable. With his comfort came some old and some new behavioral issues. It turns out Benny still can try a teacher's patience. He can run around the classroom, hit his head on a chair and end up in the nurse's office. He can refuse to write for a day and scream instead of whisper, and he can lick the dust off the computer screens. Here though, his teachers continue to teach him. They continue to see progress even as they grapple with the issues he has. Benny can still leave school each day with some accomplishment, and his teachers each day fall more in love with him. As we tried various reward strategies they switched the class teaching assistant in the hopes of finding a better fit. They brought in a psychologist to help them come up with a behavior plan. They use only positive reinforcement, and tailor it to Benny's ability to sit and focus. They speak with him, sit with him, and explain the expectations. Benny listens. The teachers realize this is a process. There are routines they will need to go through with him each day. He is trying, and each day he does a little better. He still can not always sit or control his need to be on the go, but they do not let these limitations define him. They do not use his disability as an excuse to avoid teaching him. Each day they push him further academically. After only four months in their kindergarten he can write every letter, upper case and lowercase, and can spell many words. He can do a few addition and subtraction problems.

All of this is bonus for us. I had no reason to expect him to rise to his age level academically. I wanted him in inclusion for the social role models, for the theoretical opportunity to pick up on a fraction of the traditional material. His accomplishments academically are still such a surprise for me I am not even sure what to say. He has been placed for next year in a 1st grade class with a teacher who is excited to have him. They see his progress, and they are proud to be a part of it. It is a great gift to us all.

Some nights I dream that someone will say to me that it is not working, that they can't keep teaching him, that it is too difficult or too expensive. I feel in the dream as though we are hanging precariously from a cliff, and I look down and flood with terror. I see where we could go if we should slip. The terror is short-lived because as soon as I wake up and take Benny to school I see how much Benny has become part of the fabric of the place. I see how all the teachers greet him and I see how much he is adored. Then I mainly see up. I see the sky and the clouds and the mountains ahead that we will have to climb. I look down and all I see is the soft sandy ground of the play deck. I try to look harder, below for the gorge we were over just a minute ago, but it is gone, nothing there but the slight fragrance of a nightmare. Still something is always there reminding me to be grateful, to be open, to keep working and searching for ways to help Benny continue to grow.

The more I speak with his teachers, the more it seems as if it is not such a complicated matter to teach Benny. I know that the appearance of simplicity often involves the greatest skills.

I look into the playground, I peek into the classroom, and I see my son. He is a part of the group. For a few seconds I can not even tell which little dark haired boy is mine. They mill about, jumping around like gerbils for a moment. Then for a few seconds I see him, until he falls back into the colorful lively pack.

I think back to chamber music. I am playing *Schubert's Octet*. It is my first summer at Apple Hill. It is my first experience with chamber music. I am in a group with players both more talented and more experienced than me. After the first rehearsal I wonder inside if I am ready for this group. Dobbs is our coach. We are working on the fourth movement, the variation movement. I have a few lines with the first violinist. She plays with a breathtaking sweetness. I am to blend, but also be heard. Without words, without conducting, Dobbs coaches. I weave in and out, over and under her line. I find a balance, tenuous at first, dependent on invisible forces, but over the week, I learn to find it myself. Then the next year, I work on the *Brahms Clarinet Quintet*, and I am the only woodwind in the group. Movses, our coach, asks me to become a string instrument, "in your mind," he qualifies when I look at him with questions in my eyes. Somehow I do, until the few moments when the clarinet soars above only to fall back into the rich, dense, blanket of sound, woven with a texture only Brahms could create.

I look at Benny and I become a coach inside. I hang on the corner after I drop him off, sending my vibes over the hedge and into the playground. I send over all sorts of chants, blessings, and prompts, but in the end they all carry the same message: "Blend, my child, do what the others do, but don't lose yourself."

I am conscious of the delicate balance between remaining unique and finding acceptance-the isolation of existence against the banality of conformity. These are issues we all face on some level, but these issues are magnified for those whose differences threaten to cut them off from opportunity. My eye catches Mr. R dancing as he ushers children from their cars to the entrance of the school. He seems to me to be a man of few words. Yet with all of his movements he sets a tone of acceptance, of tolerance for the quirky, and he radiates a belief that all of his students can grow.

These weeks since we have been here have taken us to a new place. The fact that Benny has begun to read and to do some basic math brings a smile to my face each day, but the major transformation, for me, stems from the sight of Benny alongside his peers. When I questioned Nancy about inclusion she told me a support network of peers would form around Benny. She explained that this network, which arises naturally from the simple act of placing a child alongside his peers, would be the primary agent for his growth. This network would take the place of some of the supports he appeared to need, and would provide him the opportunities for social growth he so badly needed. Even as she explained this to me, well after I wanted to believe her, I convinced myself that Benny would be an exception. I told myself that Benny was not disabled enough to inspire such acts of kindness. I worried that his behavior would seem merely odd and that he would turn students away rather than draw them closer. What I discovered immediately upon his entrance into his kindergarten class was that these children did not look for labels or signs. Each child, already filled with the culture of the school, flocked around him with words of support from the start. I realized that I had assumed that inclusion was powered by pity. I learned quickly that it was fueled by acceptance.

Within a few weeks, a little girl was helping him unpack his backpack, and in return Benny would push her on the swing at lunch. Benny began to lend support to his little brother, watching out for him in new ways all the time. It is this wonder that I live for each day. It is this miracle that lives and breathes within me every second of every day and night. These are the visions that are slowly replacing the nightmares I lived with for many many months.

Any parent who has worried about a child, doubted that his or her child would be able to function with others in the world, knows the content of my worst dreams. I share with you instead some snapshots of the new world in which I find myself today:

It is a day six weeks into our stay here, I pick Benny up at school. His teachers smile and one comes close to tell me that he had a "stupendous" day. He participated in class, he listened to his peers and he was good. Benny is beaming as she speaks. Then he plops his backpack heavy with books at my feet and he starts to run. He is chasing two girls, they are laughing. They make animal sounds and so does Benny. All of a sudden they are chasing him. One of them, the blond catches up and grabs Benny. The other looks sad; she wants to catch him too. Next time she does. Benny is laughing now. He runs more, he gets more animated, and he wants to make them laugh even harder. And he does. They both catch him together. They fall in a heap, covered with sand and smiles. I hold back my tears, but a few escape. Another mother talks to me. This is ordinary to her. I pretend to be in the same place. She looks at me though like she knows I am not. I like her and she likes Benny. She has three girls and we chat a bit. Soon it is time to go home. Benny picks up his backpack and tells me he ran with Laurie and Katie. He looks right into me. "I saw," I say and we walk home hand in hand.

A day just two weeks later, Benny comes out of school into the play yard and again the ordinary becomes my miracle. He comes out dancing with Julia. They are taking turns twirling each other, laughing so hard they fall over. Adam looks at me with wide eyes, glad eyes; he too knows what is special in life.

Minutes later, or so it seems, it is early morning and as we cross to the school, Laurie jumps out of her mother's car. She grabs Benny's hand and turns to me: "Ms. Linder, I'll walk Benny in today." I keep walking behind them anyway. They are only six years old, and there is an entire half a block ahead. Laurie turns again and with a partial smile says: "Don't worry; if he drops his stuff I can pick it up, I do it all the time for him." Benny now is smiling at me too, a wise sophisticated smile, for which I have no response. I keep walking behind. Then a first grade teacher stops me with her hand. She tells me to go home; she tells me Benny is fine. She explains that they are friends and that Benny pushes her on the swing during lunch. She tells me again to turn around. I stop walking forward but I can't yet turn back. Inside I am happy, outside I am lost.

And today we walk down the block plodding steadily to the main road, when Laurie runs up to Benny and stops him with a warm and cuddly hug. Benny hugs back with a gentle smile and a pinch of red flowing from his chin to his ears. Katie then comes along, puckered with jealousy, and as soon as Laurie pulls back she moves in. Another hug for Benny and he is cuddly back. She steps away; Benny stands there in momentary disbelief until he decides to finish off with a high five for them both. I look over at Benny and he has a kind smile for each of them. He looks from one to the other, almost apologetic for the rift he has unintentionally caused. I think I see that his eyes are misty. I blink and blink and find mine dry. I realize that now we have made it. We keep walking and all I can hear are soft giggles all the way to the main road.

I think I have covered all that I can. I wrote for all of the hundreds of days that ran through me with force. I wrote when I was the center, when I was the channel to Benny. Over these weeks here there has been a shift. I stood on the side for days, crying for him, laughing for him, every cell in me supporting him. Little by little he has grown these days into a little boy who can judge, react, and understand the complexities of his new and blossoming social life. I can watch today without crying, without anticipating his reactions. As close as we have been it is only now that I can step back and see him. It is maybe a set of imperceptible changes to others but one akin to his birth to me.

He was born at 36 weeks, with labored breath, absent cry and difficulty sucking. Today at age 6, 16 weeks in his new school, after 4 years of therapies, another cord was cut. We are separate in a new way now, and I can see him fully. The distance is necessary, the distance is beautiful. I am getting to know my son, and he is a rich and soulful boy. This story is a tribute to those that gave him a chance at an interpersonal life. Maybe it can be helpful to others. We need each other and we need to share our stories. Maybe someday there will be more to write, but I know now that Benny will be able to continue. Today he writes in a journal, a few sentences each morning, full, complete, thoughts, with humor, and with feeling. We have only been here for a few months. I am not quite sure where I belong yet, but I see that my child has found a place to put down his roots.

24 Letter to Nancy, August 2008

Dear Nancy,

I thought of you today because we had a garden concert here in our new backyard. My trio played all the Sphor pieces, and the Parto, and some Lachner, and a few other trios for voice, clarinet and piano. After the concert, a guest asked us to share some of our musical history. I spoke about Apple Hill and how nice it was to play outside or almost outside. I told about how I first came across the Sphor there, and I almost went into the whole story about you and how you led us to inclusion, but I stopped myself. Anyway inside I knew the rest of the story which was funny because we had a few people there who played some role in Benny's history these past few years. Some of them had not seen Benny since we moved and were amazed to find him such a talkative engaging little boy. So once again music and inclusion weave together in ways that on the outside seem coincidental, but to me reveal a hidden order to my life.

Anyway...the concert was so much fun and had a bit of the Apple Hill feel, outside, trees blowing in the wind, punch and mosquitoes and the scent of my citronella.

And Benny listened throughout, and even introduced a few pieces. He can identify all of them after a few notes. He tried to teach David the other night, but David still has trouble distinguishing Mozart from Sphor. After the concert Benny played with the children that came with their parents. He plays so beautifully now, takes turns, falls into make-believe play with ease. Just as you told me, I see now, these skills he learns best from his peers.

So please know that although I do not write every day or even every week, I think of you all the time. I hope all is well with your family. Send me an update when you have a chance.

Love,

Diane

25 One Perfect Word, February 2009

I walk into the sunlit school with ten minutes to spare before I am expected in Benny's class. Within seconds Benny's therapists and teachers find me. They all want to talk; each wants to tell me about Benny's success in their own words. They want to touch me, hug me, and connect with the mother of this child they adore. I am almost embarrassed by the attention and from their admiration. I want to tell them they have no reason to admire me, that they are the heroes today.

I have tried to tell them about the mess we faced in the city, but they do not hear me. They think it was one teacher, maybe, one bad experience, they think we just wanted the best for our son. I have tried to tell them that it was many teachers. It was the assistant principal, and the school psychologist, at not one, but two schools, who flocked around me every morning and afternoon, to tell me that my son was not functioning, and that he could not do academics.

I try to tell them that it was not a choice between good and better, it was a choice between function and disaster. They cannot understand. Their appreciation of my son is too great to allow them to glimpse the reality we faced in the city, just one year ago. They see Benny as a child with needs, but as a deeply intelligent, sensitive child. He is a child from whom they learn.

It is hard for them to imagine how misunderstood he was. Yet somewhere, I sense they see it, and their subtle awareness draws them to us with extra intensity. Do they see it in our eyes, a reflection still of the horror we faced? They must I am sure because I see it still in Benny. He has an extra reverence for those that understand him, an extra sensitivity to everyone, and a joy in being appreciated that extends beyond the expected.

I enter Benny's classroom to find all the children on the carpet. It is literacy week and parents have been invited in to read. I take out two of Benny's favorite books, and after Benny announces their titles, I read them to the class. He chose <u>Henry Hikes to Fitchburg</u>, by D.B. Johnson, and <u>My Subway Ride</u>, by Paul Dubois Jacobs and Jennifer Swender with Illustrations by Selina Alko. I read them both to a class filled with eager eyes. The children are excited to hear that Benny was born in New York City. They ask Benny questions about it as I read. They tell him about the times they rode the subway. A few children have never been on the subway and to them Benny flashes a smile of a traveler. I read for fifteen minutes and then they break up into small groups for other activities. The assistant teacher whispers again to me how well he is doing.

I walk out down the hall and look over all the "book covers" the children have made as part of the literacy week celebration. They each consist of a self portrait and a title. The title is a character trait of the child, chosen by the child. I look for Benny's. I read many until I find his. I see many titles, many of which come up frequently. I see "nice," "smart," "kind," and "athletic." They are among the most popular. Then I find Benny's. His has a title I have not seen yet. His self-portrait is there, and underneath in his slanted handwriting I see his title. He writes "Loving."

Through my entire body I feel a flood of warmth. Almost dizzy I have to anchor my feet as I adjust. I focus in on the eyes in his portrait. They belong to a boy who is understood. They belong to a boy who is accepted. They belong to a boy who is loved and is as a result very loving. The portrait drawn by Benny was created by all who have touched our lives these years. The portrait could have been different. I shudder as I think for a moment about what he would have drawn a year ago.

My eyes fall again on his word, the word he has chosen to stand for himself on this cover, on this wall of portraits, in this remarkable school. For all the limitations of language, for all the words he could not repeat, for all the silences I have learned to respect, I can not get over this word. This word says it all to me, the curve of the letters, the slant of the body, the mystery behind his choice. This word is in full glory. This word is meant to be handwritten. In all the history of the world I doubt any word ever looked so fine. I am tempted to ask him about the word, and why he chose it, but I will not. For a moment I am content to let one word define my son.

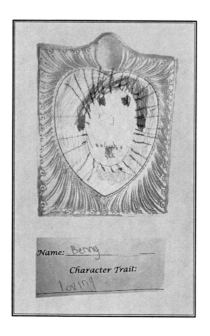

Name: Berry

Character Trait:

loving

About the Book
By Maya Memling, Psy D

When asked to write this afterword to Diane's book, I first thought, "Where do I begin?" An easy question, as I thought about it somewhat, far easier than the story that unfolds. I will tell you how I first met Diane.

Diane and I had met several years ago when we both worked in a private middle school in New York, she as a math teacher, and I as one of the school psychologists. Ours was a relationship, like many, that evolved from collaborating to help students. In this school, all teachers functioned as advisors as well as teachers and Diane was an advisor who took the struggles of her students seriously. In the course of our conversations Diane and I discovered that we worked very well together and we really liked each other, too. Both avid readers, both children of psychologists, and both walkers, we would try, when possible, to exchange lunch for a walk, to walk through the park after school. My son was growing up fast, and Diane was hoping to start a family. We were at different places in life, but found a common ground. When Diane became pregnant, I was thrilled for her.

I first saw Diane's son, Benny, on the day he was born. Diane and I had planned to top off her 37 week checkup at her obstetrician with a lunch date. But I got a call that day, canceling the lunch and telling me that he had arrived early! Excitedly, I scurried to the hospital where Diane lay, radiant, curly hairy streaming, beaming from ear to ear, having just delivered a beautiful, healthy baby boy, her husband, David, ecstatic at her side. I was thrilled to see her and to meet her new son.

What I recall the most about Benny was his hair...Benny's thick, dark shock of hair was what impressed you at first sight. There it was, in its entire newborn splendor. No bald, unformed look for this baby! He had a presence about him, and peacefulness too. Diane and David were clearly delighted to be first time parents.

And despite the fact that Diane was living in Queens at this point and I, in Manhattan, we continued to see each other after Benny's birth. This was a friendship destined to endure; we managed to get together a few times a year. When vacations rolled around, I would make sure to call Diane ahead of time to schedule a visit.

At first, it wasn't clear to me what was going on with Benny. He was quiet, and seemed language-delayed to me, but I was careful not to think in diagnostic labels or terms. I was a friend and this was a social visit. At times, nagging questions about Benny needled away at me and worried me, but I held them back. I don't think I wanted to admit that there could be something wrong. I was not the professional in this case, I thought. Speech is not my area of expertise, I rationalized to myself. And I worried about raising the specter of doubt, of being an alarmist, a know-it-all. So I basically kept quiet, listened, asked some questions and offered information that I knew when asked.

Periodically, I would hear updates. When school started, when the

evaluations unfolded, Diane began to use me as a sounding board. She would vent through late night e-mails, and within these little nuggets of communication I began to see a book in the making. I would listen, comment, gave advice when asked, but was wary about saying too much and interfering.

While I tried to avoid evaluative thoughts regarding Benny, I could not help but be impressed by the manner in which David and Diane handled the often bumpy road they had to travel through these years. I thought that Diane and David were handling this situation with a great deal of grace and intelligence. Pouring over the literature, not accepting materials or labels at face value, Diane was diligently researching treatment options and different doctors; she was vetting evaluators and therapists with a seemingly clinical acumen. I marveled also at the network of friends who came forward and gave her direction when she needed it most. I thought of those parents without these networks and began to think that Diane had to share her story. I sensed Diane would write, articulately, and with passion.

When Diane expressed concern about her ability to write an entire book, I encouraged her to try. I collected all of her notes to me, placed them in a nice new folder and took the train out to her little cottage on Long Island. We sat in between boxes, and walls in need of repair, and sifted through her "first draft." When she asked if I would be a consultant, I was flattered. I read and I questioned and I interfered. I did everything I held back from in the first place.

What developed is Benny's story, written by his mother Diane. It is an inspiring read that should be on the list for any parent or teacher of a child with special needs.

About the Team

Diane Linder is a mathematics consultant for teachers around the New York City area. She has taught both children and adults. A native New Yorker, she currently lives with her family in a suburb of New York City.

Maya Memling has worked as a psychological evaluator, taught at the university level and worked as a consultant in various schools throughout New York City.

Grace Choi is a mother, a wife, a friend, a visual artist, a pianist and a tamed cynic. She resides in New York with her husband and two boys. She loves to draw and play music together with Benny and Diane.

9 780615 333915